Top 25 locator map
(continues on inside
back cover)

◄

TwinPack
Costa Brava

TONY KELLY

Tony Kelly took up travel
writing after teaching English
in Sudan and China. He writes
regularly for newspapers and
magazines, specialising in
Spain, Croatia and family
travel. When not travelling he
lives near Cambridge, eastern
England, with his wife and son.
He has also written *AA
Essential* guides to Menorca
and Mallorca and *AA Spiral*
guides to Gran Canaria,
Portugal and Croatia.

If you have any comments
or suggestions for this guide
you can contact the editor at
Twinpacks@theAA.com

AA Publishing
Find out more about AA Publishing
and the wide range of travel publications
and services the AA provides by visiting
our website at *www.theAA.com/travel*

Contents

life *5–12*

how to organise your time *13–22*

top 25 sights *23–48*

Index *92–93*

About this book

KEY TO SYMBOLS

✚ Grid reference to the Top 25 locator map

⊠ Address

☎ Telephone number

◷ Opening times

🍴 Restaurant or café on premises or nearby

🚉 Nearest railway station

🚌 Nearest bus route

🚢 Nearest riverboat or ferry stop

♿ Facilities for visitors with disabilities

✋ Admission charge

⬌ Other nearby places of interest

❓ Tours, lectures or special events

▶ Indicates the page where you will find a fuller description

ℹ Tourist information

TwinPack Costa Brava is divided into six sections to cover the six most important aspects of your visit to the Costa Brava. It includes:

- The author's view of the Costa Brava and its people
- Suggested walks and drives
- The Top 25 sights to visit
- The best of the rest – aspects of the Costa Brava that make it special
- Detailed listings of restaurants, hotels, shops and nightlife
- Practical information

In addition, easy-to-read side panels provide fascinating extra facts and snippets, highlights of places to visit and invaluable practical advice.

CROSS-REFERENCES
To help you make the most of your visit, cross-references, indicated by ▶ show you where to find additional information about a place or subject.

MAPS
The fold-out map in the wallet at the back of the book is a large-scale map of the Costa Brava.

The Top 25 locator maps found on the inside front cover (IFC) and inside back cover (IBC) of the book itself are for quick reference. They show the Top 25 sights, described on pages 24–48, which are clearly plotted by number (**1**–**25**, not page number) in alphabetical order.

PRICES
Where appropriate, an indication of the cost of an attraction is given:
✋ Expensive, Moderate or Inexpensive.
An indication of the cost of a restaurant is given by € signs: €€€ denotes higher prices, €€ denotes average prices, while € denotes lower prices.

COSTA BRAVA
life

A Personal View

Costa Brava – the Wild Coast. The name was coined by a local journalist, Ferran Agulló, a century ago, as he gazed out at the rugged Mediterranean shore of pine-clad cliffs and coves. At times since you could be forgiven for thinking he was referring to the nightlife, rather than the scenery. When tourists started visiting Spain in the 1950s, it was to the Costa Brava that they came. Other, bigger costas followed, but it was this small corner near the French border that led the way. Fishing villages were transformed almost overnight into high-rise resorts; the face of the coastline changed more in a generation than in the previous thousand years. The Costa Brava virtually invented the sun-and-sea holiday.

Yet those rocky creeks still exist. There are villas climbing up the hillsides now, but this is still recognisable as Agulló's Wild Coast. There are areas of unspoilt marshland, Greek and Roman ruins, and long, sandy beaches with not a hotel in sight. The main city, Girona, has a charming medieval heart, and further inland are solid Catalan towns like Olot and Vic. Sheltered beneath the Pyrenean mountains in northeast Spain, the Costa Brava is part of Catalunya (Catalonia), a proud region with its own language, culture and traditions. The Catalans have a reputation for being courteous, businesslike and conservative, with little of the flamboyance of their lively Spanish neighbours. As anyone who has witnessed Carnival on the streets of Platja d'Aro will tell you, this is not entirely fair. Like all Mediterranean people, the Catalans know how to have a good time but they also know how to get things done. In recent years, Catalonia has

Pretty stone stairway at the Jardí Botànic de Cap Roig

CARNIVAL

The riotous pre-Lenten Carnival celebrations in Catalonia are among the biggest in Spain. Every town on the Costa Brava seems to organise its own Carnival festivities, with processions of floats, marching bands and participants in fancy dress. Some of the biggest parades take place in Platja d'Aro and Palamós on the weekend before Shrove Tuesday. Carnival traditionally begins with the arrival of Carnestoltes, the Carnival king, and ends with the 'burial of the sardine', a ceremony signifying the end of winter and the arrival of spring.

been granted increasing political freedom; in 2006, a referendum officially declared it a nation within Spain. The red-and-gold Catalan flag now flies above government buildings and the people look to Barcelona, rather than Madrid, as their capital. At the same time, Catalonia is enjoying a cultural renaissance, seen most visibly in the revival of the Catalan language, which has replaced Spanish as the language of everyday life. At village festivals and on warm summer evenings by the sea, people dance the *sardana*, the traditional Catalan dance in which men and women join hands in a circle symbolising the unity of the Catalan people. This authentic expression of Catalan culture was banned under General Franco, but is once again a familiar sight on the streets.

Tourism on the Costa Brava is changing too. You can still find mega-resorts like Lloret de Mar, crowded each summer with visitors from all over Europe in search of fun in the sun, but the emphasis these days is on quality as much as quantity. Manor houses and country estates are being restored as luxury boutique and spa hotels; tourists are being encouraged to visit out of season to walk, cycle and play golf. The Catalan coast is becoming fashionable once again, and pretty seaside villages like Cadaqués and Llafranc are buzzing with new restaurants and bars.

Like the new Catalonia, the Costa Brava is changing its image – no longer cheap and cheerful, but chic, confident and cool.

Flying the Catalan flag

Costa Brava's Features

GEOGRAPHY AND CLIMATE

- The Costa Brava begins at Blanes, 60km north of Barcelona, and continues around the coast for 220km to the French border at Portbou.
- There are 119 official beaches, with a total length of 56km – a quarter of the entire coastline.
- The average summer temperature is 26°C, and there are more than 200 days of sunshine a year. The sea temperature reaches 24°C in August and is pleasantly warm from June to October. The *tramuntana*, a cold north wind, can strike at any time.

GOVERNMENT AND ECONOMY

- The Costa Brava belongs to Girona province, itself part of Catalunya (Catalonia), a semi-autonomous region of Spain since 1979. Catalonia is the wealthiest region in Spain, producing 20 per cent of the country's gross national product.

PEOPLE

- The population of the Costa Brava region rises from around 425,000 in winter to a million in summer. The capital, Girona, has a population of 75,000. Catalonia has the highest population density of any region in Spain.

TOURISM

- More than five million foreign tourists visit the Costa Brava each year.
- The majority are from France, Germany and the United Kingdom. A large number of Spaniards and foreigners also own second homes in the region.
- The Costa Brava is the favourite holiday destination among Catalans, who make two million visits to the area each year.
- In the peak of the tourist season the Costa Brava can offer visitors more than 80,000 hotel beds, 100,000 pitches in campsites and 500,000 places in self-catering villas and apartments.

LANGUAGE

- Catalan has been the official language of Catalonia since 1979, though Spanish is also widely spoken and understood. Most signs and menus are in Catalan, which is used throughout this book.
- English, French and German are all widely spoken in the coastal resorts.

People of the Costa Brava

Salvador Dalí

The leading figure in the surrealist movement was born in Figueres in 1904 and had his first exhibition in 1919 in the theatre that was to become his memorial (▶ 47). After spells in New York and Paris, he returned to Catalonia and settled in Portlligat (▶ 43 with his lover Gala, whom he married in a secret ceremony in 1958. Unlike other artists, Dalí refused to go into exile during the Franco years, and in 1975 he sent the dying dictator a telegram of congratulations on the execution of five prisoners. In 1982 King Juan Carlos awarded Dalí the title of Marquis of Dalí of Púbol; Dalí responded by leaving all of his works to the Spanish state. Following Gala's death, Dalí moved into her castle at Púbol (▶ 31), but after setting fire to himself there in 1984 he lived out his remaining years in Figueres, dying in 1989 and being buried in the crypt of his museum. Dalí was a film-maker, novelist and fashion designer, but he is best known as the creator of the 'soft watch', a recurring theme from his paintings – and for the sexual obsessions which led him to recruit young models to make love while he watched.

Jordi Pujol

In 1960 a young doctor was imprisoned for organising the singing of Catalan nationalist songs during a visit by General Franco to Barcelona. Twenty years later that same man was elected President of Catalonia. The leader of the conservative Convergència i Unió party held the position for 23 years and remains a significant force in both Catalan and Spanish politics. In 2003 he was replaced by the former Socialist mayor of Barcelona, Pasqual Maragall.

FC BARCELONA

The Spanish are passionate about football, and FC Barcelona is a symbol of Catalan pride and success. 'Barça' were European champions in 1992 and 2006, but the most intense rivalry is with Spanish giants Real Madrid. Numerous foreign stars, including Diego Maradona, Johann Cruyff, Gary Lineker and Ronaldo, have been attracted to play at the Camp Nou, but the Catalan folk hero remains Ricardo Zamorra, the 'Cat', a star of the 1930s and the greatest Spanish goalkeeper of all time.

Salvador Dalí at work in his studio in 1945

A Chronology

By the 7th century BC	Iberian settlers, probably from northern Africa, establish the first towns at Ullastret and elsewhere.
550 BC	The Greeks establish trading posts at Empúries and Roses.
218 BC	The Romans land at Empúries to begin their conquest of the Iberian peninsula. Olives and vines are introduced; Catalan develops as a vernacular form of Latin.
5th century AD	Roman rule collapses and the region is occupied by Visigoths, who name it Gotalonia.
717	Muslim occupation of Catalonia. Unlike elsewhere in Spain, this lasts less than 100 years. Girona is captured by Charlemagne in 785.
878	Wilfred the Hairy becomes the first Count of Barcelona, ruling over an area roughly equivalent to modern Catalonia. Following his death in 897, his dynasty rules for 500 years.
1137	Catalonia and Aragón are united. The new kingdom becomes a major Mediterranean power, with an empire extending to Sicily, Sardinia, Malta and the Balearics. Catalan becomes the official language and the first Catalan literature is published. The Corts Catalans, with representatives from the people, the clergy and the nobility, are the first form of parliamentary government in Europe.
1469	Fernando of Aragón marries Isabella of Castile. Following the final defeat of the Moors, Aragón and Castile unite with Granada in 1492 to create modern Spain. Jews are expelled from Girona and elsewhere.
1640	The revolt of Els Segadors (the harvesters) against Spanish rule during the Thirty Years' War with France. Catalonia declares independence and places itself under the protection of the French king, finally surrendering to Spain in 1652.

1713	The Bourbon dynasty accedes to the throne following the War of the Spanish Succession. Felipe V bans the Catalan language and closes Catalonia's universities in retaliation for Catalonia supporting the Habsburg claims.
1808–14	Napoleon's troops occupy Catalonia. Girona is besieged for seven months in 1809.
19th century	Catalonia's industrial revolution makes it the wealthiest region in Spain. The cork and wine industries flourish, and Spain's first railway opens from Barcelona. Catalan nationalism is revived and there is an artistic and literary renaissance, seen in the Modernista architectural movement.
1936–39	The Spanish Civil War. Catalonia is the final Republican stronghold, but surrenders in 1939.
1939–75	Dictatorship under General Franco. The Catalan language is banned, along with traditional festivals and the *sardana* dance.
1960s	The start of the tourist boom. Girona airport is opened and new resorts are developed at Lloret de Mar and Platja d'Aro.
1975	Death of Franco. Juan Carlos becomes King of Spain.
1978	A new democratic constitution grants limited autonomy to the Spanish regions.
1979	Catalonia becomes an autonomous region, with Jordi Pujol as its president. Catalan is reinstated as the official language.
1986	Spain joins the European Community.
2003	After 23 years of conservative rule, Catalonia elects a Socialist government. Spain follows suit in 2004.
2006	A new Statue of Autonomy declares Catalonia a nation within Spain.

Best of the Costa Brava

If you have only a short time to visit the Costa Brava, or would like to get a really complete picture of the region, here are the essentials:

- Follow the winding coast road from Tossa to Sant Feliu (▶ 46), then explore the rocky coves around Begur and Palafrugell that gave the Costa Brava its name.
- Go diving or snorkelling in the clear waters around the Medes islands (▶ 35), where the reefs and caves harbour an abundance of underwater life.
- Visit the fish markets in Blanes (▶ 26), Palamós (▶ 52) and Roses (▶ 45), then dine alfresco on some of the freshest seafood you will ever eat.
- Relax in the botanical gardens at Cap Roig and Blanes (▶ 28, 26), where Mediterranean plants grow on cliffsides overlooking the sea.
- Wander the back streets of Girona, with its carefully restored Jewish quarter and medieval mansions (▶ 29, 34).
- Visit the surreal Dalí museum in Figueres (▶ 47), then follow the Salvador Dalí trail from Portlligat to Púbol (▶ 31).
- Head for one of the inland towns on market day (▶ 76) for a real taste of Catalan life. One of the best is the Saturday market at Vic (▶ 42).
- Browse in the pottery shops of La Bisbal (▶ 19, 58, 78) and take home a souvenir of your visit.
- Take a boat trip along the coast around the wild northern coastline between Roses and Cap de Creus.
- Lie on the beach soaking up the sun – the authentic Costa Brava experience. But don't forget your sunblock, water and a hat!

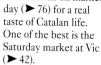

Take a dive – oxygen tanks at the ready

Sea, sun and sand at the popular resort of Llafranc

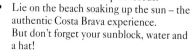

COSTA BRAVA
how to organise your time

A Walk Around Girona Old Town

This walk is best done during the early evening, when the citizens of Girona take their *passeig* along the Rambla.

INFORMATION

Distance 2km
Time 1 hour
Start/end point Pont de
Pedra
➕ C4
🚂 1km from bus and railway
station
Lunch Café l'Arcada (€)
✉ Ramba de la
Llibertat 38
☎ 972 20 10 15

Start at Pont de Pedra, the stone bridge to the north of Plaça de Catalunya. Cross this bridge to reach the old town and continue into the arcaded Plaça del Vi. Turn left and cross the square to reach Carrer dels Ciutadans.

At this point you could take one of the narrow alleys to your left to explore the medieval streets of the guilds (► 34).

Carrer dels Ciutadans leads into Plaça de l'Oli. Turn right to climb the steps towards the church of Sant Martí. Halfway up the steps, fork left beneath the arch formed by the façade of Palau dels Agullana, a handsome Gothic mansion. Continue climbing to reach Plaça Sant Domènec, dominated by its old university. Turn left to leave the square, then left again along Carrer dels Alemanys into Carrer Bellmirall.

Turn right and cross Plaça dels Lledoners to reach the cathedral's southern door. After visiting the cathedral, walk down the flight of steps beneath its main façade into Plaça de la Catedral.

Taking a break in the Plaça Sant Domenec in Girona

Turn left along Carrer de la Força. This road, and the steep, dark alleys to its left, form the heart of the atmospheric Jewish quarter (► 29). Reaching a small square, descend the steps to your right, leading to Carrer de l'Argenteria.

This smart shopping street leads into the Rambla (► 34), where you can end your walk with *tapas* and a drink beneath the arches.

A Volcanic Walk near Olot

This easy-to-follow walk provides an excellent introduction to the volcanic landscape around Olot and takes in three of its best-known features.

Start at the Can Serra car park, 5km out of Olot on the Santa Pau road. There is an information centre here where you can pick up a map of the walk. Take the underpass beneath the main road and descend the steps into the Fageda d'en Jordà beech wood.

The entire walk is waymarked with the symbol of two walkers on a red background accompanied by the number 1. The walk continues through this shady wood, joining a paved road to emerge beside a yoghurt factory before climbing sharply to the 11th-century church of Sant Miquel de Sacot.

Follow the waymarks. A short drop followed by a steep climb leads to the summit of the Santa Margarida volcano, from where an optional circular path heads down into the crater, with a small hermitage at its centre.

The path now descends to the main road, passing a farm where you can buy drinks and snacks.

Cross the road and take the lane which leads past the Santa Margarida restaurant, skirting the Volcà del Croscat. Until recently this volcano was quarried for its stone, and another optional path (No 15) leads to the scarred cliff-face where you can see the dramatic effects of the quarrying.

Continue around this volcano, and return through more beech woods, providing plenty of welcome shade, until you arrive back at Can Serra.

INFORMATION

Distance 10km plus optional extras
Time 3–4 hours
Start/end point Can Serra
➕ B2
Lunch Restaurant Santa Margarida (€)
✉ Opposite Lava campsite on the GI524
☎ 972 68 02 70

Beech trees shade the way

A Circular Walk from Tamariu

This walk begins with a short stretch of rocky coastline, before heading inland for the gentle climb to the summit of Puig Gruí (154m).

INFORMATION

Distance 8km
Time 2.5 hours
Start/end point Tamariu
➕ D4
🚌 From Palagfrugell in
   summer
Lunch Es Dofí (€€)
   ✉ Passeig del Mar 22,
   Tamariu
   ☎ 972 62 00 43

Start on the beach at Tamariu. From the southern end of the beach, near the car-parking area, cross to the smaller beach of Platja dels Liris and climb the steps, marked with red-and-white stripes, to join the GR92 coastal path.

Keep to the waymarks. You have to scramble across one rocky cove and climb around the next before levelling out on to a path running behind a stone wall.

At the next cove, climb for a few metres, then turn left through a grove of tamarisk trees. Continue to follow the red-and white-waymarks.

Eventually the path curves right, following the bend in the sea, then zigzags down to the pebble beach at the tiny cove of Cala Pedrosa.

Take the path directly behind the beach, climbing through the valley; at the top of this path turn right (leaving the GR92) to reach a road. Turn left along this road. After 50m, take the track on your right, just after a crossroads sign. The path is now marked with yellow-and-white stripes.

Off shore at Tamariu

Passing an old well and a vineyard, you climb through a tamarisk wood, with occasional glimpses of the sea to your right, until you reach the summit of Puig Gruí.

Keep to the waymarks. The path turns right and drops steeply through the forest until it reaches a road with a wide circle. Turn right and continue on this road to return to Tamariu.

A Walk Around Figueres

This short walk makes an ideal introduction to Figueres for anyone arriving by train or bus. It includes an opportunity to visit the Salvador Dalí theatre-museum (▶ 47). Start at the station. Cross the small park of Plaça Estació and fork right along Carrer Pompeu Fabra.

Turn right at the end of this street to reach the old grain market, Plaça del Gra, where a market is still held three times a week. Cross this square and take Carrer Concepció to reach Plaça de la Palmera. Turn left towards the Rambla.

A monument to Narcís Monturiol, inventor of the submarine, dominates the Rambla's eastern end. Walk down the central avenue, then take Carrer Lasauca, ahead on the left, passing the Hotel Durán, an old Dalí haunt. Cross the ring road at the end of this street to reach the tourist office in Plaça del Sol.

Continue along Carrer Mestre Falla. Take the first right to reach Parc Bosc, a shady and peaceful retreat from the crowds. After exploring the park, return to Passeig Nou and turn left. Cross the main road again and take Carrer Pep Ventura straight ahead.

Emerging on Pujada del Castell, look left for your first glimpse of the Dalí museum. Cross this street into Carrer Besalú. To visit the museum, turn left along Carrer Sant Pere; otherwise, continue straight ahead into the town hall square, Plaça Ajuntament.

Cross this square and take Carrer Peralada to reach the large ochre-coloured Modernist building, Casino Menestral. Turn right on to Carrer Ample. At the end of the street, look for the plaque opposite, denoting the house on Carrer Monturiol where Salvador Dalí was born. Turn left to return to Plaça de la Palmera and retrace your steps to the station.

INFORMATION

Distance 2km
Time 1 hour
Start/end point Figueres station
🔲 C2
🚌 To Figueres bus station on Plaça Estació
🚉 Trains from Girona and Portbou
Lunch Durán (€€)
✉ Carrer Lasauca 5
☎ 972 50 12 50

Modernist architecture fronts the Plaça Joseph Pla in Figueres

17

A Drive from Banyoles

This drive takes you into the heart of the Garrotxa, the region of dormant volcanoes just inland from Banyoles.

INFORMATION

Distance 76km
Time 2 hours, plus stops along the way
Start end/point Banyoles
✚ C3
Lunch Cal Sastrre (€€)
✉ Placeta dels Balls 6, Santa Pau
☎ 972 68 04 21

Start by the sports stadium on Carrer Alfonso XII, between central Banyoles and the lake, and take the main road heading north with the lake on your left.

After 4km this road merges with the C66 from Girona. Almost immediately you see the high peaks of the Pyrenees up ahead in the distance. Soon you reach Besalú (► 25); to explore this delightful town, park on the right, walk down to the riverbank and follow the signs to enter Besalú across the medieval Pont Vell.

Leaving Besalú, continue on the main road towards Olot.

This soon becomes the A26 motorway. When you see a tunnel ahead, take the exit on to the old N260 to Castellfollit de la Roca (► 58), perched on a ridge to your left.

Continue through this village and rejoin the A26. When the motorway ends, turn left towards Olot and keep left to skirt the city centre, following signs to Santa Pau.

Shortly after turning on to the Santa Pau road, you see the Can Serra carpark and information centre on your left. If you have time, you could stop here and do the walk described on page 15.

Sunset over the lake at Banyoles

Continue on this winding road to Santa Pau (► 59). After exploring the village, return to the same road as it twists its way down to the plain, with lovely views all the way.

Eventually you arrive at Banyoles, beside the shores of the lake.

A Coastal Drive from Lloret de Mar

This drive takes in the most dramatic stretch of coast road in the Costa Brava.

Start at the car park at the north end of the beach, beside the *sardana* statue. Take the road that leads uphill, away from the sea, and turn right at the traffic lights towards Tossa de Mar.

Once you leave Lloret the road begins to climb, and there are various *miradors* where you can pull over and admire the sea views. After passing through Tossa de Mar (➤ 48) the road twists and turns through a dizzying series of bends, with cork woods to your left and cliffs dropping into the sea on your right.

Follow this coast road for 20km, then turn right into Sant Feliu de Guíxols (➤ 46). Turn left along the seafront and left again at the end of the beach, following signs to Platja d'Aro. Pass through the centre of this resort (➤ 52–53) and continue for another 5km to Sant Antoni de Calonge, where you turn left towards Calonge.

From Calonge a minor road winds its way through the forest to the pottery town of La Bisbal (➤ 58).

Reaching the pottery town of La Bisbal, turn right towards Palafrugell. Keep on this road as it bypasses Palafrugell and continues south towards Palamós (➤ 52).

Keep going south on the coast road from Palamós, retracing your route from Sant Antoni de Calonge. The views along the corniche from Sant Feliu to Tossa are completely different when seen from the other direction, adding a further dimension to your drive.

INFORMATION

Distance 130km
Time 4 hours
Start/end point Lloret de Mar
➕ C6
Lunch Bahía (€€)
✉ Passeig del Mar 17,
Sant Feliu de Guíxols
☎ 972 32 02 19

Massive rock formations dominate the coastline from Tossa de Mar to Sant Feliu de Guíxols

19

Finding Peace & Quiet

MAR I MURTRA

The Mar i Murtra gardens at Blanes (➤ 26) make a relaxing place to spend a few hours. You can follow the guided trail around the gardens in under an hour, but bring a picnic and take your time enjoying the shady walks and views out to sea from the Linnaeus rotunda.

Take the path through one of the region's national parks

Even in the height of summer it is easy to get away from it all on the Costa Brava. There may not be room to move on the beaches, but set back from the coastline is a region of cork and oak forests, waiting to be explored. Some tourist offices issue local walking maps, and some organise guided walks in summer. The GR92 long-distance coastal footpath runs through the region, waymarked with red-and-white stripes; shorter circular routes are marked in yellow and white. For real peace and quiet, go out of season. The mild days of February, March, October and November can be perfect for walking, or even a sunny picnic on the beach. The quieter resorts have all closed down and you can have their pine-fringed coves to yourself, while towns like Blanes and Palamós have reverted to their original function as fishing ports.

NATURAL PARKS

Growing environmental awareness since the return of democracy has led to the creation of several natural parks in the region, where wildlife is protected and development carefully controlled. There are two parks on the coast – at Aiguamolls de l'Empordà (➤ 41) and at Cap de Creus (➤ 30) – as well as the offshore marine reserve around the Medes islands (➤ 35). There are also three natural parks in the inland mountains, at Serra de l'Albera, Serra de Montseny and the Garrotxa volcanic zone around Olot (➤ 15, 39). All have information centres and networks of well-marked walking trails. It is essential to keep to the paths and to avoid disturbing plants and wildlife.

FLORA AND FAUNA

The coastal region is an important breeding ground for wetland birds, especially in the Empordà marshes. Species which breed here throughout the year include purple herons, Kentish plovers, bee-eaters, marsh harriers and black-winged stilts. Flamingos, grey herons and white storks arrive during the spring and autumn migrating seasons, and in winter the lagoons are home to thousands of ducks. This is Spain's only breeding ground for the garganey, a small brown teal with blue wing panels and a distinctive striped head. Seabirds such as razorbills, gannets, storm petrels and Cory's shearwaters are attracted to the Medes islands, which also support an important colony of herring gulls.

On walks in the inland forests you may encounter red squirrels; other mammals include badgers, foxes and wild boar. Look out too for swallowtail butterflies, with their distinctive forked tails. The coastal cliffs and the Pyrenean grasslands are studded with wild flowers in spring and early summer, including asphodels, gladioli, orchids and hyacinths. Thrift and milk-vetch grow on the cliffs at Cap de Creus, where the headland is carpeted with rosemary, lavender and Spanish broom. The mountains of the Serra de Montseny are the last remaining habitat of the white-flowered saxifrage. The botanical gardens at Blanes (➤ 26) and Calella de Palafrugell (➤ 28) have impressive collections of Mediterranean flowers, plants and trees.

Flora in the Catalan countryside

Far away from the tourist mainstream

21

What's On

JANUARY *Els Tres Reis* (5–6 Jan): children across Catalonia receive their Christmas presents when the Three Kings arrive in towns and villages by boat or on horseback.

FEBRUARY *Carnestoltes*: huge, celebratory pre-Lenten carnival parades (► 7).

MARCH/APRIL *Setmana Santa* (Holy Week): on the evening of Maundy Thursday, men and boys dressed as skeletons march through Verges, near Torroella de Montgrí, performing a medieval 'dance of death'. Girona's Good Friday procession re-enacts Christ's death, with his crucified body carried to the cathedral by actors dressed as Roman soldiers. There is also a crucifixion ceremony on Good Friday in Sant Hilari Sacalm.

Festa de Sant Jordi (23 Apr): book and flower markets are set up in the streets in honour of Catalonia's patron, St George. The biggest festivities take place along the Rambla in Girona.

MAY *Carroussel Costa Brava* (Whit Sunday): Palafrugell's Spring Festival was begun in 1963 to continue the carnival traditions following its prohibition. The highlight is the parade of floats on the Sunday afternoon.

JUNE *Festa de Sant Joan* (23–24 Jun): the eve of the feast of St John is marked with bonfires and firework parties all over Catalonia.

JULY *Cantada d'Havaneres* (1st Sat): traditional sea shanties on the beach at Calella de Palafrugell.

Aplec de la Sardana (2nd Sun): the biggest *sardana* festival takes place in Olot.

Mare de Déu del Carme (16 Jul): processions of fishing boats in the main ports in honour of the protector of fishermen.

Festa de Santa Cristina (24–26 Jul): Moorish dancing and a mass pilgrimage by boat from Lloret de Mar to the hermitage of Santa Cristina.

AUGUST *Cantada d'Havaneres* (1st Sat): traditional sea shanties on the beach at Llafranc.

Mayor's Sardana (16 Aug): open spiral dance held at night in Amer, west of Girona.

SEPTEMBER *Festa del Tura* (8 Sep): processions of giants, dwarves and hobby horses in the streets of Olot.

La Diada (11 Sep): Catalonia's national day is marked all over the region by fireworks, street parades and *sardana* dancing.

COSTA BRAVA's
top 25 sights

The sights are shown on the maps on the inside front cover and inside back cover, numbered **1**–**25** alphabetically

Aiguablava

The original Costa Brava bay is still a beautiful spot, and a reminder of what this coastline was like before the advent of tourism.

It was here, in 1908, that the journalist Ferran Agulló first coined the term *costa brava*, and the rocky coves around Begur retain much of their ruggedness today. Of course they have now been discovered by tourists, and luxury 'urbanisations' are creeping up the hillsides, but out of season you can still have pine-fringed cliffs, golden sand and sparkling turquoise bays (Aiguablava means 'blue water') to yourself.

The bay at Aiguablava is dominated, unusually, by an ugly white *parador*, a state-run hotel, built on the cliffs to take advantage of the view. Across the bay is the chic resort of Fornells, little more than a marina, a smart hotel and a pair of tiny beaches. North of here are more small coves – Sa Riera, with views over the Medes islands, and Aiguafreda and Sa Tuna, linked by a footpath cut into the rock.

The pretty cove of Aiguablava

Besalú

A well-preserved medieval town centre at the heart of the region, with several Romanesque churches and the only Jewish bathhouse in Spain.

This small town at the confluence of the Fluvià and Capellada rivers was the historic capital of the Garrotxa region, ruled for more than 200 years by a dynasty established by Wilfred the Hairy. After the 12th century its importance declined, but following its declaration as a National Historic Monument in 1966 it has been restored to its former glory.

Come here on a Tuesday morning, when the porticoed central square, Plaça Llibertat, is buzzing with chatter and the market stalls are piled high with flowers, fruit and cheese, and you realise that this is still very much a working town. Along the cobbled streets which fan out from the square are delicatessens and antiques shops, set among medieval arches, columns and Gothic windows. Of several Romanesque churches, the most impressive is the monastery church of Sant Pere, with a pair of stone lions adorning its façade.

The symbol of Besalú is its angled bridge over the Fluvià, built in the 11th century and destroyed several times, most recently in the Spanish Civil War. Arriving by car, park on the Banyoles side and enter Besalú across the bridge. Near here is the Miqvé, the only remains of a once significant Jewish community. This ritual bathhouse, with thermal springs and running water from the river, was used by men before prayer and by women before marriage, childbirth and menstruation. The tourist office arranges guided visits.

INFORMATION

- 🔲 B2
- 🍴 Choice of restaurants and cafés (€–€€)
- 🚌 From Figueres, Girona and Olot
- 🔄 Plaça Llibertat 1
  ☎ 972 59 12 40
- ℹ️ Castellfollit de la Roca (► 58)
- ❓ Market on Tue; Festa dels Dolors, evening procession on the Fri before Palm Sunday; *sardana* dancing on Easter Sunday; Festa Major, last weekend in Sep.
  A 1-hour miniature train tour in summer includes a guided walk and visit to Miqvé

Besalú's 12th-century fortified bridge

Blanes

INFORMATION

- C6
- Restaurants (€–€€€)
- From Figueres and Girona
- From Girona and Lloret de Mar
- To other south coast resorts in summer
- Passeig de Catalunya 2
  ☎ 972 33 03 48
- Lloret de Mar (➤ 36)
- Market on Mon

Mar i Murtra

- ✉ Passeig Karl Faust 9
- ☎ 972 33 08 26
- 🕐 Jun–Sep daily 9–8;
  Apr–May, Oct daily 9–6;
  Nov–Mar daily 10–5
- None
- From Plaça de Catalunya
- Few
- Moderate

Blanes is where it all begins. The Costa Brava starts at the rocky promontory of Sa Palomera and continues north all the way to France.

Climb on to Sa Palomera, halfway along the beach, for some of the best views of Blanes. South of here, the beach stretches on, as far as the eye can see, passing hotels, campsites and the mouth of the River Tordera at the start of the Costa Maresme. To the north, a wide promenade with gardens, play areas and restaurant tables on the street leads around to the town's attractive, and still busy, fishing harbour.

Blanes is still a working fishing port, where the arrival of the fleet each evening is followed by an animated auction in the fish market – you can watch it all happening from the upstairs bar. Fishermen mend their nets, old men sit on the sea walls and the sailors' chapel of Nostra Senyora de l'Esperança is adorned with nautical themes. Blanes may be one of the Costa Brava's largest resorts, but with a population of more than 20,000 it has managed to absorb the tourists without losing its soul.

The old town, just behind the seafront, has survived almost unscathed, with Gothic churches, medieval houses, fountains, shrines and a lively daily produce market. Just above the town is the Mar i Murtra botanic garden, dramatically situated on a clifftop, with collections of cactus, palms and aloe and a charming Mediterranean garden.

Crowds gather at Blanes' fish auctions

The road beyond the gardens continues to the small beach at Cala Sant Francesc, where there is a beach bar in summer. You can also walk or drive from the gardens to the Castell de Sant Joan, an 11th-century castle and 15th-century hermitage with sweeping views of the town's beach.

Cadaqués

This fishing village and stylish resort has long attracted a curious mixture of artists, tourists and people seeking an alternative way of life.

Cadaqués appears at first sight to be a typical Mediterranean fishing village. It still is a fishing village, but it is much more than that. Picasso spent some time here in the early 20th century, but it was Salvador Dalí who really put Cadaqués on the map. His father came from here; it was here that he met his wife; and it was near here, at Portlligat, that he eventually settled down, attracted by the light, the remoteness and the rugged beauty of Spain's most easterly village.

There are reminders of Dalí everywhere: a statue on the seafront, a sundial on the façade of a hotel, the logo of the L'Hostal bar. In the 1960s, when hippies and intellectuals flocked to Dalí's side, Cadaqués was known as Spain's St Tropez. It holds the same appeal for many people today.

There are several art galleries and stylish boutiques. The Museu de Cadaqués features contemporary Catalan artists. The old town of steep and narrow streets winds its way from the waterfront up to the church of Santa Maria, with its baroque reredos.

INFORMATION

- D7
- Wide choice of restaurants and bars (€–€€€)
- From Figueres and Roses
- Carrer Cotxe 2A
  ☎ 972 25 83 15
- Cap de Creus (➤ 30), Portlligat (➤ 43)
- Market on Mon; Mare de Déu del Carme, procession of fishing boats on 16 Jul; international music and arts festival, Jul and Aug

Museu de Cadaqués

- ✉ Carrer Narcís Monturiol 15
- ☎ 972 25 88 77
- ⊘ Hours vary according to exhibition. Usually summer 10.30–1.30, 4–8
- 💰 Moderate

A view over the rooftops at Cadaqués

Calella de Palafrugell

INFORMATION

➕ D4

🍴 Several beachside
restaurants (€€)

🚌 From Palafrugell

🔄 Llafranc (➤ 52)

❓ Festival of *havaneres*,
first Sat in Jul

Jardí Botànic

✉ Cap Roig, 4km from village

☎ 972 61 45 82

🕐 Apr–Sep daily 9–8;
Oct–Mar daily 9–6

💶 Moderate

❓ Costa Brava Jazz Festival
held each Jul and Aug

*The Jardí Botànic de Cap
Roig near Calella de
Palafrugell (above)*

This pleasant resort is made up of a series of coarse, sandy beaches attractively strung out beneath an old fishing village.

The village now includes a few whitewashed holiday villas, but it has lost none of its original charm. You can still see working fishermen here, and fishing boats on the sand add a splash of colour to the scene. The people of Palafrugell and beyond head to Calella at weekends to eat at the waterfront seafood restaurants, while their children play on the beach.

Calella de Palafrugell is the setting for one of the Costa Brava's more unusual festivals each July, when popular musicians gather to sing *havaneres* on the beach. These melancholy sea shanties, brought back from Cuba by Spanish sailors and rooted in the Creole music of the Caribbean, have been sung in the fishermen's taverns of Calella for at least 100 years. They are best enjoyed while drinking *cremat*, a local concoction of coffee, rum and cinnamon, which is served flambéed.

A cliff path from Calella leads around to the next bay at Llafranc. At the other end of the village, high above the bay, is the Jardí Botànic de Cap Roig, a beautiful garden laid out in 1927 by a White Russian emigré, Colonel Nicolai Woevodsky, and his English wife, Dorothy Webster. There are cypress, cork oak and mimosa trees and hundreds of Mediterranean plants, tall cedars and pine trees, bent by the wind and leaning towards the sea as if paying homage to the Mediterranean.

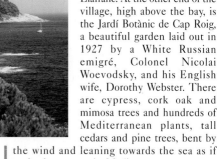

*Sailing out from Calella
de Palafrugell*

Call Jueu, Girona

The dark, narrow, steep streets of the ancient Jewish ghetto form one of the most atmospheric quarters of Girona, well worth a visit.

For six centuries until their expulsion in 1492, Girona was home to one of the largest Jewish communities in Spain. At one time, up to 1,000 Jews lived in the area around Carrer de la Força, where there were three synagogues, a Jewish school, a ritual bath and a Jewish butcher.

The Call (Jewish ghetto) was sealed off for many years, but it has recently been opened up, allowing visitors to explore its fascinating web of narrow alleys and stone steps. The hidden courtyards and gardens of the Call hold many dark secrets, and the streets echo with the suffering of the Jewish people down the years.

At the centre of the Call is the Centre Bonastruc Ça Porta. This Jewish museum and cultural centre is named after the founder of the Cabbalist school of Judaism, also known as Rabbi Nahmánides, born in Girona in 1194. Cabbalism is a secret system of mysticism, metaphysics and mathematics, which claims to read hidden messages into the scriptures.

The Museu d'Història dels Jueus tells the tragic story of Catalonia's Jews, persecuted for 300 years before being finally driven out. Among the exhibits are tombstones from the Jewish cemetery on Montjuïc, the 'mountain of the Jews' overlooking Girona. The poignant Hebrew inscriptions on the tombstones are truly touching in their simplicity.

INFORMATION

🔹 C4
🍴 El Pou del Call, Carrer de la Força (€€)

Museu d'Història dels Jueus
✉️ Carrer de la Força 8
☎️ 972 21 67 61
🕐 May–Oct Mon–Sat 10–8, Sun 10–3; Nov–Apr Mon–Sat 10–6, Sun 10–3
♿ None
💶 Inexpensive

Architectural gem on the old walls of Girona

Cap de Creus

INFORMATION

🔲 D1

🍴 Restaurant Cap de Creus
(€€)

🚌 Cadaqués, 8km away

↔️ Cadaqués (➤ 27),
Portlligat (➤ 43)

❓ *Sardana* dancing at
sunrise on 1 Jan

**Parc Natural de Cap
de Creus**

ℹ️ Palau de l'Abat, Monestir
de Sant Pere de Rodes

☎ 972 19 31 91

🕐 Daily 10–2, 3–6

❓ Walking and cycling trails
from Sant Pere de Rodes

*The stunning Cap de
Creus peninsula*

**This jagged peninsula, where the
Pyrenees jut into the sea, is a place of
savage beauty and vicious winds making
you struggle to stay on your feet.**

Salvador Dalí lived just down the road at
Portlligat (➤ 43), and as you stand on the headland gazing down into secluded creeks it is
impossible not to see Dalíesque images in the
rocks, carved by nature into ever more surreal
shapes. This is where the *tramuntana*, the
legendary north wind that strikes fear into sailors
and fishermen, is at its most violent.

The easiest way to reach the cape is from
Cadaqués (➤ 27), on a narrow road which
snakes across the headland. There is also a
coastal footpath from Portlligat, difficult to
follow but with the reward of seeing this craggy
landscape at its isolated best and dipping into
hidden coves along the way. The road ends at a
lighthouse, where you can walk on to the slate
cliffs and look down over the seascape of deep
turquoise water, small islands and rocky coves.
This is the easternmost point in mainland Spain
and if you come here at dawn
you can watch the sun rise over
the Iberian peninsula. Seabirds
migrate here in winter and
wheatears and rock thrushes
build their nests in spring,
when the cliffs are carpeted
with wild flowers and the
headland is scented with
rosemary and lavender. Swifts
and pipits arrive in summer. In
1998 the entire headland was
designated a protected nature
reserve, with its headquarters
in the former abbot's palace at
the monastery of Sant Pere de
Rodes (➤ 37).

Castell Gala Dalí, Púbol

The castle which Salvador Dalí bought as a refuge for his wife has become a shrine to her memory and to the couple's bizarre relationship.

When Salvador and Gala Dalí were in exile in Italy during the Spanish Civil War, the painter promised his wife that he would one day buy her a castle. Thirty years later he acquired this Gothic and Renaissance castle in the village of Púbol. Dalí wanted Gala to be able to get away from him, with her lovers if necessary, and insisted that he would never enter the castle without her permission.

The castle was in a state of disrepair and Dalí set about re-creating it. The result is a typically Dalíesque mixture of the grotesque, the beautiful and the absurd. Classical statues in the garden share space with elephant figures sculpted from cement; 17th-century tapestries hang beside *trompe l'oeil* painted radiators and huge Dalí canvases. Everywhere you look there are portraits of Gala, and her initial G is frequently worked into the design.

Gala spent little time in her castle, arriving for short stays each summer but continuing to live with Dalí in Portlligat. When she died in 1982 her body was driven to Púbol and buried in the crypt – with a stuffed giraffe looking on. Dalí moved into her room, but two years later he set fire to the bed and, despite a life-saving operation, he was never to return to the castle. The Cadillac in which he insisted on leaving Púbol – he refused to take an ambulance – still sits in the garage. Dalí left the castle to the Spanish state and it was opened to the public as a museum in 1996.

INFORMATION

- C4
- ☎ 972 48 86 55
- 🕐 15 Jun–15 Sep daily 10–8; 15 Mar–14 Jun, 16 Sep–1 Nov Tue–Sun 10–6; 2 Nov–31 Dec Tue–Sun 10–5
- 🍴 Can Bosch (€) in village
- 🚌 Buses between Girona and Palafrugell pass about 2km away
- ♿ Separate wheelchair entrance
- 💶 Moderate

The crypt (above) and ornate fountain (below) at Castell Gala Dalí

Catedral, Girona

INFORMATION

🔳 C4
✉ Plaça de la Catedral
☎ 972 21 44 26
🕐 Apr–Oct daily 10–8;
  Nov–Mar daily 10–7
♿ None
💵 Moderate (free on Sun)

Girona's cathedral is one of the great churches of Spain, a triumph of architectural styles coming together to create a unifying and satisfying whole.

The cathedral was begun in 1312 on the site of an earlier church. The best way to approach it is via the huge rococo staircase leading up to its Renaissance façade, an exquisite piece of stone carving with floral reliefs and sculptures of saints supporting the central rose window.

Access through the main door is for services only; visitors should enter through a separate door to the left. The entrance ticket gives access to the cathedral itself as well as the treasury and cloisters, and includes the use of an audio guide. Inside, the cathedral is dominated by its single Gothic nave, at 23m the widest in Europe. Other features to look out for include the 11th-century alabaster altarpiece and the embossed silver canopy above the high altar.

Finely carved entrance to the cathedral at Girona

The Treasury contains two real gems. One is an illustrated 10th-century manuscript of the Beatus, or Commentary on the Apocalypse. The other is the 11th-century Tapestry of the Creation, once used for teaching the scriptures to illiterate adults and children. It features vivid portraits of the changing seasons, the sun, moon, stars, animals and fish, with Adam, Eve and the angels woven around the central figure of Christ. Don't miss the 12th-century Romanesque cloisters, with a view of the original bell-tower, Torre de Carlemany, skilfully incorporated into the 14th-century Gothic design.

Empúries

An ancient Greek and Roman settlement on the shores of the Gulf of Roses, where Spain first came into contact with wider European culture.

It was the Greeks who first established a trading post (*emporion*) here on what was then an island; contact between Greek settlers and indigenous tribes led to the development of the Iberian culture. The Romans anchored at Empúries in 218BC, the first step on the route to the colonisation of Spain. The Roman city of Emporiae was abandoned in the 3rd century AD and only rediscovered by archaeologists in 1908. Much of it has still to be excavated.

The remains of the Roman city show how much Spanish town planning owes to Roman influence. The forum at the centre, the forerunner of the Plaça Major, would once have been surrounded by arcades; there were temples at one end and a main street leading to the city walls. Even the amphitheatre outside the walls has its equivalent in today's bullring or football stadium. Some of the Roman villas have well preserved mosaic floors.

Below is the Greek city, dominated by a statue of Asklepios, the god of healing (the original is in Barcelona's archaeological museum). A small museum interprets the ruins, and there is an excellent audio-visual show. Afterwards you can walk along the seafront, past the original Greek jetty, to the village of Sant Martí d'Empúries, site of the first Greek settlement.

INFORMATION

- ✚ D2
- ✉ 1km north of L'Escala
- ☎ 972 77 02 08
- 🕐 Jun–Sep daily 10–8; Oct–Mar daily 10–6. Closed 1 Jan, 25 Dec
- 🍴 Snack bar (€) on site, restaurants (€–€€) in Sant Martí d'Empúries
- 🚌 To L'Escala from Figueres, Girona and Palafrugell
- ♿ None
- 💶 Inexpensive

Remains of Roman villas in Empúries

Girona Old Town

INFORMATION

* C4
* Choice of restaurants (€–€€€)
* Girona, 1km away
* Girona bus station, 1km away
* Rambla de la Llibertat 1
  ☎ 972 22 65 75
* Holy Week procession on Good Friday

The narrow alley, Carrer de la Força in Girona's old town

The restoration of the old quarter at the heart of Girona has been one of the great success stories of modern Catalonia.

Girona is a city for strolling, wandering at random among the maze of streets and going wherever a hidden archway or flight of steps leads you. Sun and shade, iron and stone, courtyards and balconies, narrow alleys and wide open squares, all come together here in perfect harmony.

Girona is at its most enchanting in the streets of the old guilds. Between Plaça de l'Oli and Plaça del Vi, once the oil and wine markets, lies a network of narrow lanes, each named after a medieval trade. Carrer de l'Argenteria was once lined with silversmiths, Carrer de Mercaders with merchants, Carrer de les Ferreries Velles with blacksmiths and Carrer Peixateries Velles with fish-mongers. Their places may have been taken by trendy cafés and boutiques, but the streets are still appealing.

The Rambla beside the River Onyar is the hub of Girona's social life, and the best place to see it all is from one of the cafés beneath the vaulted arches. The Pont de Pedra, the stone bridge at the top of the Rambla, looks down over the river, with its iron and wooden bridges and brightly painted tenement houses backing on to the water. One of the bridges, the Pont de les Peixateries, cuts directly through the houses and on to the Rambla. It was built for the city by the French firm of Eiffel and Company, creators of the famous tower in Paris.

Illes Medes

This offshore archipelago and marine nature reserve is a magnet for diving and snorkelling, and also attracts a wide variety of fauna and flora.

Seven rocky islets, a continuation of the Montgrí massif, harbour a rich diversity of plant and animal life, and in 1985 they were declared Spain's first marine nature reserve. Local fishermen, banned from fishing in the area, feared for their livelihood; but the protection of the marine environment has been such a success that catches are up everywhere else as a result. Scuba-divers come from all over Spain to swim among coral reefs and caves teeming with grouper, scorpion fish and spiny lobsters. Glass-bottomed boats leave regularly in summer from the harbour at L'Estartit (▶ 52); some trips include the opportunity to go snorkelling. There are strict regulations about fishing, boating and night diving in the protected area, and it is essential to check with the authorities at the harbour in L'Estartit. In the past the islands have been used as a pirate hideout and a French military prison, but nowadays they are uninhabited – apart from the seabirds, especially the thousands of yellow-legged gulls, which breed here between March and May each year.

INFORMATION

🏠 D3
🛈 Carrer Eivissa, L'Estartit
☎ 972 75 11 03
🚤 Trips from L'Estartit in summer and occasionally on winter weekends
🔄 L'Estartit (▶ 52)

Take a trip on a glass-bottomed boat (above) to the Illes Medes (below)

Lloret de Mar

You'll either love it or hate it – the tourist capital of the Costa Brava is a big, brash holiday resort with more hotel beds than Barcelona.

Modernist decoration on the church of Santa Roma in Lloret de Mar

Fifty years ago Lloret de Mar was still a fishing village; now it has been transformed into a pulsating resort whose population rises to 200,000 in summer and where it is easier to get a hamburger than a Spanish meal. The main thoroughfare, Carrer la Riera, is a non-stop strip of discos, bars and amusement arcades, busy day and night. Since the 1990s there have been attempts to change Lloret's image, but that seems to be missing the point. If you want fun in the sun, there's no better place. The main attraction is the long sandy beach. There is good sheltered swimming at the northern end, beneath the mock castle overlooking Sa Caleta cove. Near here is a monument to the *sardana*, the Catalan national dance, designed by local sculptor Domènec Fita in 1971. A cliff path from the southern end of the beach leads to another popular landmark, the bronze sculpture of the *Dona Marinera* (fisherman's wife) by Ernest Maragall. The path continues to Cala Banys, a rocky inlet with a beach bar in summer. Further south, the beach at Santa Cristina is the setting for a traditional festival each July, when the people of Lloret make a pilgrimage by boat, carrying a statue of their patron saint to the hermitage bearing her name.

The old town lies just behind the promenade. Look for the 16th-century parish church, with its unusual Modernista (art nouveau) mosaic roof. Also of interest is Can Garriga, a colonial-style mansion built in 1887 by a wealthy merchant returning from Cuba. It now houses the tourist office and the Museu del Mar, the maritime museum. The square outside is the venue for occasional performances of *sardana* dancing on summer evenings.

Monestir de Sant Pere de Rodes

This former Benedictine monastery in the hills above Cap de Creus has long been a place of pilgrimage, as much for its views as anything else.

Some claim that the monastery was built on the site of a Roman temple, but the more colourful story concerns Pope Boniface IV (608–615) and St Peter's head. With Rome under threat, the Pope ordered the church's most sacred relics to be sent to Spain for safe keeping. When the time came to retrieve them, the head was nowhere to be found, so a monastery was built on the site here and dedicated to the saint. There are records of a monastery here from AD878 – though recent excavations suggest that the site was in use long before that. The present church, dating from 1022, marks the transition to Romanesque architecture in Catalonia. The original cloister, its galleries decorated with murals, is covered by an upper cloister on the same level as the church. This was an important place of pilgrimage throughout the Middle Ages, but fell into decline after the 14th century. The last monks left in 1798.

There are good views of the monastery from the chapel of Santa Elena, all that remains of the village which grew up around the church. For the best views, climb the path behind the monastery to the ruined castle of Sant Salvador. Look down over the monastery and out to sea, then turn to see the Pyrenees on the horizon. The sunrises up here – some of the first in Spain – are magical.

INFORMATION

- 🔲 D1
- ☎ 972 38 75 59
- 🕐 Jun–Sep Tue–Sun 10–7.30; Oct–May Tue–Sun 10–5
- 🍴 Cafe-restaurant (€)
- 🚉 Vilajuïga (8km)
- 🚌 El Port de la Selva (5km)
- ♿ None
- 🎫 Moderate (free on Tue)
- ↔ El Port de la Selva (➤ 53)

Wind your way up to the monastery

Museu Episcopal & Catedral, Vic

Fine examples of paintings in the museum (above and below)

The cathedral and episcopal museum at Vic form a unique treasury of Catalan religious art stretching back almost a thousand years.

Vic's cathedral was begun in the 11th century, but the present building dates from 1803, when the Romanesque bell-tower was incorporated into a new neoclassical design. Parts of the original cloister survive, with a 14th-century Gothic cloister on top. The most unusual feature is the set of wall paintings by the Catalan mural artist Josep Maria Sert. His first paintings were damaged by fire during the Spanish Civil War and the replacements were inaugurated only days before his death in 1945. The striking red and gold colours and apocalyptic biblical scenes form a powerful link between the persecution suffered by Christ and that felt by Catalonia at the hands of Spain. Sert is buried in the cloisters. A few of the remaining pieces from his first decoration of the cathedral are displayed in the Capella de la Pietat, a baroque chapel on Carrer Cardona.

The town's diocesan museum contains more than 20,000 exhibits, including the most complete collection of Catalan Romanesque art outside Barcelona. The treasures on display include frescoes and altarpieces from remote Pyrenean churches, and some wonderfully lifelike 12th-century wooden statues of the Virgin. Also here are Gothic religious paintings by some of Catalonia's finest artists, including Lluís Borrassa, Bernat Martorell and Jaume Huguet. The museum is housed in a magnificent new building which opened next to the cathedral in 2002.

Olot

The capital of the Garrotxa region is a truly Catalan town which manages to be both industrious and stylish, conservative at heart with a radical edge.

The people of Olot have a strong sense of Catalan identity: you are unlikely to hear anyone speaking Spanish. This Catalan spirit is openly displayed at the town's two biggest festivals – the Aplec de la Sardana, on the second Sunday in July, when visitors come from all over Catalonia to perform the *sardana* dance; and the Festa de la Tura, on 8 September, when figures of giants and hobby-horses parade through the streets.

Olot was a centre of textile production, and an art school was opened here in the 18th century. A century later, one of its pupils, Joaquim Vayreda, helped to found the Olot School of painters. The romantic scenes of rural life produced by these early Catalan impressionists were influenced by the European trends of the time, yet rooted in the Garrotxa landscape of volcanic hills.

The smart shopping streets of the old town around the Plaça Major lead to the neoclassical parish church of Sant Esteve. Near here is the start of the Rambla, also named Passeig Miquel Blay, after a well-known Olot sculptor. This delightful promenade, with coffee tables beneath the trees, contains some unusual Modernist architecture, as well as the imposing 19th-century Teatre Principal. The Rambla is also the venue for Olot's lively market, which takes place regularly on Monday mornings.

INFORMATION

➕ B2
ℹ️ Carrer de l'Hospici 8
☎ 972 26 01 41
🔁 Santa Pau (▶ 59)

Dusk arrives at the town of Olot

Pals

This carefully restored hilltop village is like an open-air museum, with fortified towers, cobbled streets and views over the Empordà plain.

This walled village of Gothic stone houses around a 15th-century castle was abandoned in 1939 after the Spanish Civil War, but it was slowly and lovingly restored after 1948. Many of the houses are now second homes for people from Barcelona. At times the village is too pretty for its own good – numerous galleries and pottery shops testify to its popularity with tourists – and to appreciate it at its best you should come in the early morning or the evening, when the sunlight is at its most subtle and you can enjoy the alleys and archways without the crowds. The long, sandy beach of Platja de Pals, with modern holiday facilities, is 5km away on the coast.

A short drive from Pals leads to Peratallada (➤ 59), another restored medieval village set around an 11th-century castle. Take the bridge across the moat to enter the village, then wander the back streets around the attractive, arcaded Plaça de les Voltes.

Colourful flowers enhance the medieval stone walls in Pals

Parc Natural de l'Aiguamolls de l'Empordà

This wetland nature reserve provides a refuge for wildlife and migrant birds and a peaceful haven for visitors escaping from the crowded beaches.

Once upon a time, marshes covered the coastal plain; Empúries (▶ 33) was an island and the Montgrí mountains were surrounded by fens. As the population grew, the marshes disappeared, at first as a result of agriculture and lately because of tourism. The building of the marina on former marshland at Empúriabrava, galvanised environmentalists into action, leading to the creation of this natural park in 1983.

Carp, mullet and eel thrive in the lakes; there are badgers, newts and voles, and otters are being reintroduced. Above all the Empordà marshes are an important refuge for aquatic and migrant birds. Herons, ducks and geese live on the ponds; other species that breed here include the stone-curlew and the black-winged stilt. This is Spain's only nesting ground for the garganey, a rare species of duck. Seabirds flock here in winter, and during the main migrant seasons (Mar to May and Aug to Oct), it is possible to see 100 species in a day.

At the information centre in El Cortalet you can pick up leaflets and maps, and hire binoculars, field guides and wheelchairs. There are two easy, waymarked trails from here, with hides overlooking the lagoons; except during the nesting season (April to mid-June) they can be combined with a walk along the beach in a two-hour circular trail.

The main settlement of the reserve is Sant Pere Pescador, a peaceful village of farmers and fruit-growers on the banks of the River Fluvià. The biggest attraction is its beach, a long and lonely stretch of sand on the shores of the Gulf of Roses, with campsites among the dunes. Out of season you can have views of the bay to yourself.

INFORMATION

⊞ D2

El Cortalet

✉ Off the road from Castelló Empúries to Sant Pere Pescador

☎ 972 45 42 22

🕓 Trails open at all times

🍴 None

🚃 Castelló d'Empúries

♿ Good

💲 Free (charge for car parking)

❓ Keep to the paths at all times; be prepared for flooding in winter

ℹ Information centre: Apr–Sep 9.30–2, 4.30–7; Oct–Mar 9.30–2, 3.30–6. Closed 1 Jan, 25 Dec

Walking and birdwatching are popular pursuits in the park

Plaça Major & Market, Vic

INFORMATION

✚ A4
ℹ️ Carrer de la Ciutat 4
☎ 938 86 20 91
🍴 Cafés and bars around the edge of the square (€)

The opening of the C25 highway has brought the ancient market town of Vic, with its attractive medieval centre, within easy reach of the coast.

Vic's main square is one of the most perfect in Catalonia, where buildings of different styles and ages come together, linked by the uneven arches around their base, to create a satisfying whole. This has always been, above all else, a market place; but to experience its symmetry and beauty, come back when it is empty. Within the square are the Gothic town hall, begun in 1388, and buildings from the Renaissance, baroque and Modernist periods.

The best time to visit Vic is on a market day (Tuesday or Saturday), when the main square, Plaça Major, is buzzing with life. Fruit and vegetables are sold at one end, flowers at the other, while the arcades around the edges shelter everything from baby chicks to second-hand books. Stalls at the centre of the square sell bric-à-brac, pottery, household utensils and cheap clothes, and a crafts and wholefood market is set up in the neighbouring square, Plaça del Pes. The butchers and sausage-makers on Carrer dels Argenters do a brisk business (Vic has long been renowned for its *fuet* and *botifarra* sausages) and the streets of the old town echo with gossip. By 3pm the bars are full and the market has been cleared away; by 4pm the cleaners have done their job, the cafés have put out their chairs and you can sit in the sun and appreciate Plaça Major as it is the rest of the week, with pigeons in the square, children playing in the sand and no sign that a market has taken place at all.

Markets have been held twice a week in Plaça Major ever since the 10th century. The biggest market, Mercat del Ram, takes place on the Saturday before Palm Sunday.

Spicy sausages for sale in the town of Vic

Portlligat

The house where Salvador Dalí lived out his fantasies is a typically Dalíesque mixture of the kitsch, the beautiful and the absurd.

This small fishing village on the outskirts of Cadaqués (► 27), with boats moored on the beach and the gentle waters of the bay enclosed by an offshore island, is where the painter Salvador Dalí made his home. Attracted by the Mediterranean light and by memories of idyllic childhood holidays in Cadaqués, he first moved here with his future wife Gala in 1930 and stayed permanently from 1948 until her death in 1982.

His house, Casa-Museu Dalí, built over the ruins of a pair of fishermen's cottages, is full of quirky Dalíesque touches – eggs on the roof, camels in the garden, plant pots in the shape of teacups and a swimming pool modelled on the Alhambra in Granada. In 1997 it was opened to the public, largely as Dalí left it, and a visit here provides a fascinating insight into the artist's troubled mind.

From the moment you are greeted in the entrance hall by an enormous stuffed polar bear, Dalí's creative genius is at work. The tour of the house includes the artist's studio and bedroom, with a mirror carefully positioned so that the first sunlight in Spain would fall on Dalí's bed. Afterwards, you can stroll through the garden and climb the hill above the house for views over the bay.

Only a few visitors are allowed in at a time, so booking is essential. In summer it is also possible to take a trip on Dalí's old fishing boat, *Gala*, passing isolated coves on the way to Cap de Creus (► 30).

INFORMATION

🟥 D1
🍴 Chez Pierre (€€)
🚏 Cadaqués
🔄 Cadaqués (► 27),
   Cap de Creus (► 30)

Casa-Museu Dalí
✉ Portlligat
☎ 972 25 10 15
🕐 15 Jun–15 Sep daily
   9.30–9; 15 Mar–14 Jun
   and 16 Sep–6 Jan
   Tue–Sun 10.30–6
💶 Expensive
❓ Advance booking is
   essential. Boat trips daily
   10–8 in summer
   ☎ 617 46 57 57

Casa-Museum Dalí – the surreal former home of artist Salvador Dalí

Ripoll

INFORMATION

➕ A2

🍴 Restaurants and cafés
(€–€€)

🚌 From Girona and Olot

❓ Market on Sat; wool
festival, first two weeks
in May

Monestir de Santa Maria

✉ Plaça Abat Oliba

🕐 Daily 10–1, 3–7

💶 Inexpensive

*Market day at Ripoll
(above); the elaborate
doorway of the Santa
Maria monastery (below)*

**This small town in the Pyrenean
foothills grew up around its monastery,
which contains one of the greatest
treasures of Catalan Romanesque art.**

Wilfred the Hairy, the first Count of Barcelona,
used Ripoll as a base from which to unite the rival
factions of the southern Pyrenees, following the
reconquest of Catalonia from the Moors. He
founded the Monestir de Santa Maria in 879 on
the site of an earlier Visigothic church. During its
golden age in the 11th and 12th centuries, the
monastery ruled over an area stretching from
Barcelona into modern France and became a
great centre of European learning. Most of the
church was destroyed by fire during the dissolu-
tion of the monasteries in 1835, but the great
west portal survived. This is one of the jewels of
Catalan Romanesque architecture, its pillars and
arches covered in vivid reliefs of Biblical stories,
zodiac signs and scenes from agricultural life.

The 12th-century cloisters of the
monastery church have also
survived, with expressive faces on
the sculpted capitals. The nearby
Museu Etnogràfic has everything
from matchboxes and cowbells to
Civil War posters gathered
together by a local historian.

The nearby town of Sant Joan
de les Abadesses was founded by
Wilfred the Hairy, who
established the convent here as a
gift for his daughter. Other sights
include the arcaded main square
and the bridge over the River Ter
at the entrance to the town. You
can get there on the 12km
Vía Verde cycle route, which
follows the disused railway line
from Ripoll.

Roses

A fishing port and ancient Greek colony, Roses has become the tourist capital of the northern Costa Brava, ideal for family holidays.

With 4km of sandy beach at the head of a great sweeping bay, Roses is the perfect setting for a bucket-and-spade holiday. The sheltered waters are ideal for water sports, with windsurfing, sailing and waterskiing all available. There are also several smaller coves, beginning with Canyelles and Almadrava, 3km beyond the fishing harbour to the southeast. A hair-raising drive across a rugged landscape leads to the remote creek of Cala Montjoi; on the way you pass the Creu d'en Cobertella, the largest prehistoric burial chamber in Catalonia, dating from 3000BC.

Roses was founded in the 8th century BC by Greek settlers, who named it Rhodes after their homeland, but it was the Romans who developed the fishing industry which led to the town's wealth. It is still an important fishing port, with a population of 12,000, which rises to 80,000 in summer. With 50 hotels, five campsites and dozens of restaurants and bars, it is a little too lively for some; but if you want a traditional beach holiday, with easy access to the quieter north coast, this is the best place.

The star-shaped Citadel (Ciutadella) at the entrance to town is a 16th-century fortress on the site of the original Greek city, with Roman and medieval remains within its walls – you can clamber over the ruins and look down into the moat. Another ruined castle, east of town, stands on the slopes of Puig Rom hill. Climb this hill at sunset for romantic views over the Bay of Roses with the snow-capped Pyrenees in the distance.

INFORMATION

- D2
- Wide choice of restaurants and cafés (€–€€€)
- From Cadaqués and Figueres
- Trips to Cadaqués and Cala Montjoi in summer
- Cadaqués (► 27)
- Market on Sun; Mare del Déu del Carme, procession of fishing boats on 16 Jul
- Avinguda de Rhode 77
  ☎ 972 15 05 37

Ciutadella de Roses
- Apr–Sep daily 10–8; Oct–Mar Tue–Sun 10–6
- Inexpensive

Ruins of the Citadel (top) and the beach (above) near the town of Roses

Sant Feliu de Guíxols

Handsome Modernist mansions line the promenade of this attractive seaside town, where tourism dates back more than a hundred years.

This used to be the Costa Brava's busiest resort. It's an unexpectedly handsome and dignified town, where most of the building took place before the 1960s high-rise boom. Fishing and boatbuilding are important industries, and during the 19th century the town grew rich on the export trade in cork. The elegant Modernist buildings on the seafront are a reminder of this wealth: look out for Casino la Constancia, a Moorish-style edifice with arches, mosaics and turrets and an old-style café on the ground floor.

Sant Feliu grew up around its Benedictine monastery, of which all that remains is the Porta Ferrada, a pre-Romanesque atrium with horseshoe arches. The same complex of buildings includes the parish church, built over the monastery ruins, and a small museum of local artefacts and archaeological finds.

The main beach is a wide arc of sand with a fishing harbour at its north end. From the beachfront promenade, Rambla Vidal, with its toy museum (▶ 57), leads into the old town of narrow streets and squares. The market square contains an unusual 1929 market hall, with art deco touches and bright stained glass. From the southern end of the beach, a road climbs 2km to the chapel of Sant Elm. A tourist 'train' makes the trip up regularly during the summer.

The monastery (above) and the beach (below) at Sant Feliu de Guíxols

Teatre-Museu Dalí

The memorial which Salvador Dalí created for himself in his home town of Figueres is a journey through the imagination of a tortured genius.

This is one of the most visited museums in Spain – but is it really a museum at all? Dalí, its creator, denied that it was, calling it 'a gigantic surrealist object'. Even the name theatre-museum has two meanings. It is built on the ruins of an old theatre, where Dalí had his first exhibition at the age of 14; but it is also a theatre because of the way we are meant to respond. Dalí did not want captions, or a catalogue; he wanted the 'audience' to be free to create their own surrealist experience.

From outside, the view is dominated by the transparent dome on the roof, together with Dalí's trademark eggs on the façade. Once inside, you are drawn to the courtyard, with its central sculpture, *Rainy Taxi*, featuring a giant model of Dalí's wife Gala standing on a black Cadillac. Some things you cannot miss – like the Mae West room, where a sofa and two fireplaces are turned by means of a lens into a pouting face. Sooner or later you reach the crypt, where Dalí is buried; Dalí spent his last years in the Torre Galatea, and on his deathbed told the Mayor of Figueres that he

wanted to be buried in his theatre, rather than with Gala in her castle at Púbol. A separate exhibition dedicated to Dalí's jewellery is now open, complete with paintings of his designs.

INFORMATION

✠ C2
✉ Plaça Gala-Salvador Dalí 5, Figueres
☎ 972 67 75 00
🕐 Jul–Sep daily 9–7.15; Oct–Jun Tue–Sun 10.30–5.15. Closed 1 Jan, 25 Dec
🚉 Figueres 1km away
🚌 Figueres bus station, 1km away
♿ Few
💶 Expensive
❓ Night-time opening in Aug 10–12.30

Weird and wonderful shapes at the Teatre-Museu Dalí

Tossa de Mar

INFORMATION

- C6
- Restaurants (€–€€)
- From Lloret de Mar (and Girona in summer)
- South coast resorts in summer
- Lloret de Mar (➤ 36)
- Market Thu
- Avinguda del Pelegrí 25
  ☎ 972 34 01 08

Museu Municipal
- ✉ Plaça Roig i Soler 1
- ☎ 972 34 07 09
- ⏰ Jun–Sep daily 10–8;
  Oct–May Tue–Sat 10–2,
  4–6, Sun 10–2
- Inexpensive

The remains of a fortified medieval village look down on a horseshoe beach, making Tossa the most attractive of the Costa Brava resorts.

One resort on the crowded southern coast stands out head and shoulders above its neighbours. The beach alone would be enough to draw visitors, with safe swimming and sheltered sunbathing in an idyllic bay, and several smaller coves within easy reach. But what makes Tossa special is its walled medieval village (Vila Vella), standing proudly above the bay as it has done for more than 800 years.

Climb up from the main beach, Platja Gran, pausing to glance back at the sea through the arched window of an abandoned church, and you soon reach this attractive village. It was established in 1186 by the Abbot of Ripoll on the promontory of Mont Guardí. Beneath here, just behind the beach, is the Vila Nova (New Town), a warren of back streets and 19th-century houses around the parish church.

Tossa was one of the first places on the Costa Brava to attract foreign visitors. The painter Marc Chagall spent the summer of 1934 here and called it his 'blue paradise'. The Museu Municipal, in the former Abbot's palace, contains letters from Chagall, who was delighted that the museum was to display one of his paintings, *The Celestial Violinist*. Tossa's most recent attraction is the interesting Mediterranean Lighthouse Interpretation Centre, which opened in 2005 in an old lighthouse at the summit of Vila Vella. The views from here along the coast are spectacular, and there is an enjoyable interactive museum with videos and special effects.

Crystal clear waters at Tossa de Mar

COSTA BRAVA's
best

Historic Sights

PASSEIG DE LES MURALLES, GIRONA

This walkway, along the medieval ramparts, offers marvellous views over the city. It begins near Plaça de Catalunya and continues past the convent and university of Sant Domènec to the ruined watchtower, Torre Gironella. For the best views, climb onto some of the newly restored towers, from where the distant peaks of the Pyrenees are visible on a clear day. The walk ends at Passeig Arqueològic, a series of attractively landscaped gardens between the cathedral and the River Galligants.

➕ C4 🕐 Daily 8am–10pm
💲 Free

BANYS ÀRABS (ARAB BATHS), GIRONA

The so-called Arab Baths are a 13th-century Romanesque creation, based on an earlier Moorish design and influenced by Roman styles. Nevertheless, they are one of the best preserved medieval bathhouses in Spain and are definitely worth a visit.

➕ C4 ✉ Carrer del Rei Ferran el Catòlic 🕐 Apr–Sep Mon–Sat 10–7, Sun 10–2; Oct–Mar daily 10–2 ♿ None 💲 Inexpensive

CASTELL DE SANT FERRAN, FIGUERES

This star-shaped citadel, begun in 1753 as a defence against the French, was once claimed to be the second-largest fortress in Europe. During the Napoleonic Wars it was captured by French forces, who imprisoned and later executed the hero of the Girona resistance, Alvarez de Castro. In 1939, it became the final bastion of Republican forces during the Spanish Civil War. On a one-hour, self-guided audio tour, you can stroll around the ramparts and visit the parade ground, chapel and vaulted stables. Even when it is closed you can get a feel for its vast size by walking around the 3km path that encircles the castle walls.

➕ C2 ✉ Pujada del Castell ☎ 972 50 60 94 🕐 1 Jul–15 Sep daily 10.30–8; 16 Sep–30 Jun daily 10.30–3 ♿ None
💲 Inexpensive ❓ Jeep tours of ramparts, dinghy trips of underground cisterns at weekends and summer – reservations essential

ULLASTRET

Archaeological excavations at Ullastret have revealed most of what we know about the ancient Iberian culture, which thrived here between the 6th and 2nd centuries BC. It developed in the late Bronze Age as a result of contact between early Greek settlers and native populations, and is considered to be the first indigenous culture of modern Spain. The Iberian settlement at Ullastret is the largest yet discovered in Catalonia. This fortified village was built on what was, at that time, an island on a marshy lake. Parts of the walls and the defensive towers remain, together with public buildings including cisterns, grain stores and temples to an unknown god. The village was abandoned in the 2nd century BC, following the Roman occupation of Empúries (► 33), and was deserted until excavations began in 1947.

➕ D4 ✉ Puig de Sant Andreu ☎ 972 17 90 58 🕐 Easter and Jun–Sep Tue–Sun 10–8; Oct–May Tue–Sun 10–2, 3–6 🏠 In nearby village of Ullastret ♿ Access to museum, but site is uneven
💲 Inexpensive (audio guide extra) 🔄 La Bisbal (► 58)

Octagonal pool in the Banys Àrabs

Activities

CYCLING
The network of greenways on Catalonia's disused railway lines includes the narrow-gauge routes from Olot to Girona and Sant Feliu de Guíxols.

DIVING AND SNORKELLING
The best area is around the Medes islands nature reserve (➤ 35). For a full list of diving schools, contact Costa Brava Sub (☎ 972 751768; www.subcostabrava.com).

FISHING
Licences are required for sea and river fishing – local tourist offices can give details and may be able to issue fishing permits.

GOLF
There are ten golf courses in the Costa Brava, with more under development. There are also a number of pitch-and-putt courses (➤ 82).

HORSE RIDING
There are riding schools in most of the main resorts, with tuition for beginners and more advanced riders.

SAILING
There are 17 marinas between Blanes and Portbou, ranging from Aiguablava (62 moorings) to Empúriabrava (5,000), and the calm waters make perfect sailing conditions.

SKIING
The twin resorts of La Molina and Masella offer the biggest ski area in the Pyrenees. Other popular winter sports centres are Camprodon and Vall de Núria, near Ripoll.

SWIMMING
There are more than 30 Blue Flag beaches between Blanes and Portbou, offering clean water and safe swimming whenever the green flag is flying.

WALKING
The GR92 coastal path runs the length of the Costa Brava. There is also good hiking in the Garrotxa volcanic zone, Cap de Creus nature park and the Serra de l'Albera mountains.

WINDSURFING
You will find windsurfing schools in all the main resorts, but the best conditions are in the Bay of Roses and at Platja de Pals.

PARACHUTE JUMPS
The skydiving centre at Empúriabrava aerodrome has become the largest in Europe. Beginners can take a tandem jump, accompanied by a professional instructor, with a 15-minute flight followed by an exhilarating freefall from 4,000m. Prices start at around €150, with the additional option of having the experience recorded on camera or DVD.
☎ 972 450111; www.skydiveempuriabrava.com

The Costa Brava provides the perfect venue for water sports

Beaches & Resorts

LLAFRANC

Pine trees shade a beachfront promenade and yachts flutter in the small marina beside a perfect bay, where tamarisks grow out of the rocks around an arc of fine sand. Although this resort has grown more popular in recent years, the development is restrained and few of the buildings are more than two or three storeys high. A coastal path leads to Calella de Palafrugell (➤ 28), or you can walk or drive up to the lighthouse at Cap de Sant Sebastià for views back over Llafranc.

🔢 D4 🍽 Several good restaurants (€€) 🚌 From Palafrugell 🔄 Calella de Palafrugell (➤ 28), Tamariu (➤ 53) ❓ Festival of *havaneres* on the beach, first Sat in Aug; annual festival 29–31 Aug

Boats are the order of the day at Palamós

L'ESTARTIT

What was once little more than a fishing harbour, serving the nearby town of Torroella de Montgrí (➤ 59), has grown into a bustling, modern holiday resort with a reputation for nightlife and a thriving water sports industry. The main attraction here is the beach, which stretches for 5km and is backed by a seafront promenade. This is a good resort for families with young children – the water is shallow, the sand shelves gently and a miniature train trundles along the seafront. Unlike some of the larger resorts to the south, L'Estartit virtually closes down in winter, when all the locals retreat to Torroella de Montgrí.

🔢 D3 🍽 Choice of restaurants and cafés (€–€€€) 🚌 From Girona and Torroella de Montgrí 🚢 Trips from Cadaqués and Palamós in summer 🔄 Illes Medes (➤ 35), Torroella de Montgrí (➤ 59)

PALAMÓS

In the 19th century Palamós was the chief export harbour for Catalonia's cork industry, and despite the growth of tourism the town retains a significant commercial base today. The fishing fleet still sails every day from Palamós and its arrival each afternoon is followed by a lively fish auction by the harbour. The old quarter, dominated by the Gothic church of Santa Maria, stands on a headland overlooking the harbour. Several shops here specialise in cork artefacts from the continuing small-scale cork industry. A former warehouse on the dockside houses the Museu de la Pesca (Fishing Museum), with exhibits exploring the town's seafaring traditions. The museum offers boat trips around the bay.

🔢 D5 🍽 Restaurants (€–€€€) 🚌 From Girona, Palafrugell and Platja d'Aro 🚢 To other south coast resorts in summer 🔄 Platja d'Aro (➤ below) ❓ Market on Tue; carnival, week before Lent

PLATJA D'ARO

The small fishing harbour of the village of Castell d'Aro grew over the last 50 years into the Costa Brava's second largest resort, with a population that rises from 3,000 in winter to more than 100,000 in summer. The beach is 3km of golden sand, the nightlife is legendary and there are numerous activities for children. From discos to water sports, whatever you want in Platja d'Aro is probably there – except peace and quiet. The original village survives 3km inland, with a medieval castle where art exhibitions are sometimes held, and a Museu de la Nina (Doll Museum, ➤ 57). For those who want to escape from the beach, there are free guided walking tours of the old village throughout the year.

🔢 D5 🍴 Wide choice of restaurants (€–€€€) 🚌 From Girona, Palafrugell and Platja d'Aro 🚢 To other south coast resorts in summer 🔗 Palamós (➤ 52), S'Agaró (➤ below) ❓ Market on Fri; carnival, week before Lent ℹ Carrer Verdaguer 4 (☎ 972 81 71 79)

EL PORT DE LA SELVA

With its whitewashed houses facing an attractive harbour, this small resort on the edge of the Cap de Creus peninsula looks every bit the timeless Mediterranean fishing village that it almost is. Fishing boats still set out each day to gather the anchovies for which El Port de la Selva is known, but fishing is slowly giving way to tourism. The water is shallow, the beach is long and sandy, and there is good windsurfing in the sheltered bay. The Serra de Roda mountains, with the monastery of Sant Pere de Rodes (➤ 37) looking down, provide the perfect backdrop.

🔢 D1 🍴 Restaurants and bars on the waterfront (€–€€) 🚌 From Cadaqués, Figueres and Llança 🚢 Excursions to Cap de Creus 🔗 Monestir de Sant Pere de Rodes (➤ 37) ❓ Market on Fri

S'AGARÓ

This exclusive villa development, on a headland between the beaches of Sant Pol and Sa Conca, was begun around 1924, when industrialist Josep Ensesa commissioned Girona architect Rafael Masó to design the first houses. Built in his classical *noucentista* style, the resort is an attractive mix of Italianate villas, landscaped gardens and a coastal promenade around a succession of rocky coves. Masó's work was completed in the 1940s by Francesc Folguera, who designed the neo-baroque church at the centre of the resort. Film stars and politicians have long flocked to S'Agaró's famous hotel, Hostal de la Gavina, designed by Masó as a Gothic villa and given a more austere classical style by Folguera.

🔢 D5 🍴 Beachside restaurants at Platja Sant Pol (€€), Hostal de la Gavina (€€€) 🔗 Platja d'Aro (➤ 52), Sant Feliu de Guíxols (➤ 46)

TAMARIU

Named after the tamarisk trees that once surrounded its bay, Tamariu is the smallest and prettiest of the three resorts on this stretch of coastline near Palafrugell. In recent years it has become decidedly chic, and many of the old fishermen's cottages have been turned into holiday homes for Catalan families from Girona and Barcelona. The main beach, a crescent of golden sand, is backed by a wide pedestrian promenade lined with seafood restaurants. A short walk around the headland to the north leads to the rocky cove of Aigua-xelllida, with its own small beach.

🔢 D4 🍴 Seafood restaurants (€€–€€€) 🚌 From Palafrugell in summer 🔗 Aiguablava (➤ 24), Llafranc (➤ 52) ❓ Festival of *havaneres* on the beach, first Sat in Sep

The wide sandy beach at S'Agaró

53

Museums

MUSEU D'ART, GIRONA

This museum in the former episcopal palace contains a large collection of Catalan art, from Romanesque to contemporary. Among the exhibits to look for are the 10th-century portable altar from the monastery of Sant Pere de Rodes (➤ 37), the 14th-century stencils used to design stained-glass windows for the cathedral in Girona, and the scenes of 20th-century Girona by the Catalan artist Santiago Rusinyol and the Polish painter Mela Mutter.
➕ C4 ✉ Pujada de la Catedral 12 ☎ 972 20 38 34
🕐 Mar–Sep Tue–Sat 10–7, Sun 10–2; Oct–Feb Tue–Sat 10–6, Sun 10–2 ⚕ Very good – wheelchair access and braille panels
♿ Inexpensive

CASAL DES VOLCANS, OLOT

The Garrotxa region around Olot has been at the centre of volcanic activity for hundreds of thousands of years. Although the most recent eruption was more than 11,000 years ago, the volcanoes are still officially considered dormant, rather than extinct. Nor are volcanoes the only threat. A major earthquake struck the city in 1427, and there were tremors at nearby Besalú as recently as 1988. This museum, housed in a Palladian villa inside the botanic gardens at Parc Nou, explores the history and geology of the volcanic region, as well as its fauna and flora. The information centre for the Garrotxa natural park, in an office above the museum, is a good place to pick up leaflets about the area and walking maps and guides. A waymarked walk (No 17) leads to the Volcà de Montsacopa, a typical volcano just north of the town centre. You can get there just as easily by following the signs from the Museu Comarcal, from where it will take around 20 minutes to reach the crater. Pass market gardens on the lower slopes, then walk uphill through an avenue of plane trees lined with Stations of the Cross. From the chapel of Sant Francesc, on the summit, there are marvellous views. You can walk right around the rim of the crater, or follow the path down to its floor.
➕ B2 ✉ Avinguda de Santa Coloma (1km from town) ☎ 972 26 67 62 🕐 Tue–Fri 10–2, 3–6, Sat 10–2, 4–7, Sun 10–2 🍴 Café (€)
♿ Good ♿ Inexpensive

MUSEU ARQUEOLÒGIC, GIRONA

This archaeological museum, in the 12th-century Romanesque monastery of Sant Pere de Galligants, contains a collection of artefacts, from prehistoric to medieval times. Among the finds are Roman pottery and mosaics from Empúries (➤ 33) and three Roman milestones indicating the distance to Gerunda – the Roman name for the city. The cloister is notable for its beautifully sculpted capitals of mythological and biblical figures.
➕ C4 ✉ Plaça de Santa Llúcia ☎ 972 20 26 32
🕐 Jun–Sep Tue–Sat 10.30–1.30, 4–7, Sun 10–2; Oct–May Tue–Sat 10–2, 4–6, Sun 10–2 ♿ Good ♿ Inexpensive

Fine examples of Catalan art displayed in Girona's Museu d'Art

MUSEU DE L'ART DE LA PELL (LEATHER MUSEUM), VIC

Tanning is one of Vic's traditional industries, and this museum, housed in a former convent, contains an unusual collection of leather artefacts from around the world. There are chopstick holders from China, funerary face masks from Cameroon, embossed armchairs from Portugal, suitcases from Peru, shadow puppets from Thailand, religious paintings from Spain and a riding saddle from Mexico.

➕ A4 ✉ Carrer Arquebisbe Alemany 5 ☎ 938 83 32 79 🕐 Tue–Sat 11–2, 5–8, Sun 11–2 ♿ Good 💵 Free

MUSEU COMARCAL DE LA GARROTXA, OLOT (GARROTXA COUNTY MUSEUM)

Housed in an 18th-century hospice, the museum contains the most important collection of work from the Olot School of painters. Key figures in the movement were Josep Berga i Boix (1837–1914) and Joaquim Vayreda (1843–94), with many of Vayreda's paintings of rural life on display. The Modernist sculptor Miquel Blay was also influenced by the Olot School; among his works is a portrait of Berga i Boix. More modern work includes a selection of nudes by the sculptor Josep Clarà, a pupil of Berga i Boix. The museum also includes displays on Olot's traditional industries – bell-making, clog-making, textiles and religious statuary.

➕ B2 ✉ Carrer de l'Hospici 8 ☎ 972 27 91 30 🕐 Tue–Fri 10–2, 3–6, Sat 10–2, 4–7, Sun 10–2 ♿ Good 💵 Inexpensive

MUSEU DE L'EMPORDÀ, FIGUERES

The museum of local art and history was established in 1876 and moved to its present site on the Rambla in 1971. It contains archaeological discoveries from the Iberian, Greek and Roman periods, and a collection of 19th- and 20th-century Catalan art. There are several paintings by Antoni Tàpies, one by Dalí and a lithograph donated by Joan Miró. Artists from Figueres are well represented in the section on Empordan realism.

➕ C2 ✉ Rambla 2 ☎ 972 50 23 05 🕐 Tue–Sat 11–7, Sun 11–2 ♿ Few 💵 Inexpensive (free with entrance ticket for Dalí museum)

MUSEU D'HISTÒRIA DE LA CIUTAT, GIRONA

The city museum, in the former Capuchin monastery of Sant Antoni, details the history of Girona from prehistoric times to today. Among the more unusual exhibits, the ground-floor display on industrial history features an old petrol pump, wireless sets and an early computer. Upstairs, there is a room devoted to the development of the *sardana* dance. The cemetery of the original convent is preserved just inside the entrance, with niches on the walls designed for mummified corpses.

➕ C4 ✉ Carrer de la Força 27 ☎ 972 22 22 29 🕐 Tue–Sat 10–2, 5–7, Sun 10–2 ♿ None 💵 Inexpensive

MUSEU ARQUEOLÒGIC, BANYOLES

Located in the pleasant town of Banyoles (► 58), this museum is in the 14th-century almshouses in the old part of town. It gives an insight into the ancient prehistory (both archaeology and palaeontology) that is so rich in this area. A copy of the jawbone of a pre-Neanderthal man is kept in the museum. The orginal, at least 100,000 years old, was discovered in 1887.

➕ C3 ✉ Plaça de la Font 11 ☎ 972 57 23 61 🕐 Jul–Aug Tue–Sat 10.30–1.30, 4–7.30, Sun 10.30–2; Sep–Jun Tue–Sat 10.30–1.30, 4–6.30, Sun 10.30–2 💵 Inexpensive

Children's Attractions

LOOKING AFTER CHILDREN

Small children are particularly vulnerable to the sun and need to be well protected. Apply a high-factor sun block regularly, especially after swimming, and keep their heads covered during the heat of the day. If you rent a car, make sure that it has a child seat – book this in advance and check it carefully on arrival. The same goes for cots and high-chairs in hotels and apartments.

Most children are happy enough just playing on the beach – and the Costa Brava's beaches are perfect, with safe, shallow water, lots of sand and Red Cross posts in case of emergency. You can buy beach toys in all the resorts and rent pedaloes on most of the beaches. Although swimming is generally safe, the larger beaches operate a flag system and you should never let young children in or near the sea when the red or yellow warning flags are flying. The green flag means that it is safe to swim, but currents change quickly and you should still take care.

Off on a boat trip to the Illes Medes

AMUSEMENT PARKS

GNOMO PARK

Little children will love this 'gnome farm', which offers mini-golf, an adventure playground, bouncy castles, train rides and a woodland trail – and, of course, lots of gnomes!

✚ C6 ✉ Carretera de Lloret, near Blanes ☎ 972 36 80 80 ⏰ Easter–Oct Tue–Sun 11–9; Nov–Easter Sat–Sun 11–9

MAGIC PARK

Funfair and indoor play area with roller-skating, a miniature boating lake, inflatable toys, dodgem cars, a carousel, video games and a soft play area for younger children. There is another Magic Park located in Lloret de Mar.

✚ D5 ✉ Avinguda S'Agaró 86, Platja d'Aro ☎ 972 81 78 64 ⏰ Daily 10am–1am

ANIMALS

PARC ANIMAL DE SOBRESTANY

Wildlife park with deer, bison, wild boar, ostriches and Pyrenean sheep. There is a walking trail and a driving tour where you are given a bag of feed for the animals.

✚ D2 ✉ Camí de Sobrestany, between Torroella de Montgrí and L'Escala ☎ 972 78 84 94 ⏰ Daily 9–8 summer, 10–6 winter

BOAT TRIPS

THE NAUTILUS ADVENTURE

Children will enjoy any boat trip on the Costa Brava, but this one is extra-special as it travels out to the Medes Islands in boats with submerged cabins, allowing you to observe the fish swimming along the seabed.

✚ D3 ✉ Passeig Marítim 23, L'Estartit ☎ 972 75 14 89 ⏰ Departures several times a day in summer and at winter weekends, depending on the weather

MUSEUMS

MUSEU DEL CINEMA, GIRONA

The history of moving images, from Chinese shadow puppets to the latest films – covering some 500 years.

✚ C4 ✉ Carrer Sèquia 1 ☎ 972 41 27 77 ⏰ May–Sep Tue–Sun 10–8; Oct–Apr Tue–Fri 10–6, Sat 10–8, Sun 11–3

MUSEU FAUNA SALVATGE, OLOT

Conjure up the sounds and sights of Pyrenean wildlife at the touch of a button at this interactive 'zoo'.

✚ B2 ✉ Carrer Dr Zamenhoff ☎ 972 27 26 49 ⏰ Daily 9–9

MUSEU DEL JOGUET DE CATALUNYA, FIGUERES

More than 3,000 traditional children's toys are on
display here, including toy soldiers, model trains and a
teddy bear which once belonged to Salvador Dalí's
sister.

➕ C2 ✉ Carrer Sant Pere 1 ☎ 972 50 45 85 ⏰ Jun–Sep
Mon–Sat 10–7, Sun 11–6; Oct–May Tue–Sat 10–6, Sun 11–2

MUSEU DE LA JOGUINA, SANT FELIU DE GUÍXOLS

A charming collection of vintage toys, including
rocking horses, beach toys and model trains, on display
in a Modernist town house.

➕ D5 ✉ Rambla Vidal 48–50 ☎ 972 82 22 49 ⏰ Jul–Sep daily
10–1, 5–9; Oct–Jun Tue–Fri 10–1, 4–7, Sat 10–1, 4–8, Sun 11–2

MUSEU DE LA NINA (DOLL MUSEUM), CASTELL D'ARO (NEAR PLATJA D'ARO)

A collection of more than 300 dolls, made from
different materials and from all parts of the world.

➕ D5 ✉ Plaça Lluís Companys ☎ 972 81 71 79 ⏰ Mon–Fri 6–9,
Sat–Sun 11–1, 6–9 in summer; Sat–Sun 11–1, 5–9 in winter

WATER PARKS

AQUABRAVA

Waterslides, beaches and the biggest wave pool in
Europe are among the attractions on offer.

➕ D2 ✉ Carretera de Cadaqués, Roses ☎ 972 25 43 44
⏰ Jun–Sep daily 10–7 🚌 Free bus from Roses and Empúriabrava

AQUADIVER

Children who enjoy messing about in water, will love
this – wave machines, zigzagging toboggans, rapids
and a 'kamikaze' free-fall ride.

➕ D5 ✉ Carretera Circumval.lació, Platja d'Aro ☎ 972 82 82 83
⏰ Jun–Sep daily 10–6 (Jul–Aug 10–7) 🚌 Free bus from Platja
d'Aro, Palamós and Sant Feliu de Guíxols

MARINELAND

Aquatic park with dolphin and sea-lion shows and a
small zoo with penguins and seals. Thrill rides include
the Black Hole, Boomerang and Twister.

➕ C6 ✉ Carretera Malgrat a Palafolls, near Blanes ☎ 937 65 48
02 ⏰ May–Sep daily 10–6,
(Jul–Aug 10–7) 🚌 Free bus from
Blanes, Lloret de Mar and Tossa de Mar

WATER WORLD

Pools, slides and the Water
Mountain, where you can
take a big-dipping roller-
coaster ride.

➕ C6 ✉ Carretera Vidreres, Lloret
de Mar ☎ 972 36 86 13 ⏰ Mid-
May–Sep daily 10–6 (Jul–Aug 10–7)
🚌 Free bus from Blanes, Lloret de
Mar and Tossa de Mar

MINIATURE TRAIN RIDES

In addition to the attractions
listed, children will enjoy the
miniature road train rides in
summer at Girona, Besalú,
Banyoles, Cadaqués, Blanes,
Lloret de Mar, Tossa de Mar,
Sant Feliu de Guíxols and Vic.

PORT AVENTURA

One of Europe's top theme
parks is situated within reach
of the Costa Brava, around
two hours' drive south of
Girona at Salou. Port Aventura
is divided into five fantasy
lands representing different
areas of the world, together
with roller coasters, thrill rides
and spectacular shows. The
same complex includes the
Caribe waterpark. Get there by
taking the AP-7 motorway via
Barcelona and leaving at
junction 35. Port Aventura is
open from 10–7 daily from
late March to early November,
with extended opening to
midnight in July and August.
☎ 977 779090;
www.portaventura.es

*Daring exploits for all the
family at Water World*

57

Towns & Villages

CASTELLFOLLIT DE LA ROCA

Spectacularly perched on a 1km-long basalt promontory, carved out by the River Fluvià, this village looks for all the world as if it is about to fall off the cliff. The best view is from below, as you approach Castellfollit on the road from Besalú. At night, the cliff is floodlit and you can pick out the different geological layers in the rock. The narrow streets of the village, their houses built from volcanic stone, converge by a church, where you can gaze 60m down into the precipice below. Castellfollit is known for its almond biscuits and its pork sausages, and in the Museu d'Embotit (Sausage Museum ✉ Carretera Girona 10 🕐 Daily 💶 Free) you can taste the local products after looking at old-fashioned mincing machines and models of the *matança* or annual slaughter of pigs.

➕ B2 🍴 Fonda Ca La Paula on main street (€) 🚌 From Besalú, Figueres, Girona and Olot

BANYOLES

The capital of the Pla de l'Estany county makes a pleasant place to while away a summer afternoon. The main square, Plaça Major, is a perfect example of the genre, with three- and four-storey houses climbing above the ground-floor arcades. Just outside Banyoles is a lake, fed by an underground spring, where the 1992 Olympic rowing contests and the 2004 World Championships were held. This is where the locals come to have fun in summer – you can swim, fish, rent a rowing boat or walk the 8km around the lake's shore. Check out the Museu Arqueològic (➤ 55), located in the 14th-century almshouses in the centre of town.

➕ C3 🍴 Restaurants (€–€€) 🚌 From Besalú, Girona and Olot

BEGUR

This hilltop town with a ruined 15th-century castle would make a good base for exploring the rocky coves around Aiguablava (➤ 24). Narrow streets fan out from the church square, and you can climb to the castle for marvellous views stretching north along the coastline as far as the Bay of Roses.

➕ D4 🍴 Several restaurants and bars (€–€€) 🚌 From Girona and Palafrugell ❓ Market on Wed

LA BISBAL

La Bisbal is best known as the centre of the Catalan ceramics industry. Its most abiding image – and the only one that many visitors see – is of the dozens of pottery shops lining the Girona road. A twin-arched bridge leads over the River Daró into the old town, which comes alive each Friday with one of the region's busiest markets. The Romanesque bishops' palace, on the old town square, is a reminder that this quiet county town was once the seat of the bishops of Girona.

➕ D4 🍴 Choice of restaurants and cafés (€–€€) 🚌 From Girona and Palafrugell ❓ Market on Fri

CASTELLÓ D'EMPÚRIES

Castelló d'Empúries was the seat of the Counts of Empúries during the Middle Ages and many of its buildings date from that time. Its greatest glory is the basilica of Santa Maria, an early Gothic church built on the site of a Romanesque cathedral and considered the second church of Girona province, after Girona Cathedral itself. Other buildings of note are a 14th-

Colourful ceramics on sale at La Bisbal

century prison and the El Rentador wash house, with a porticoed atrium, a fountain and a view of the basilica through its arches. Close by is the resort of Empúriabrava, built in 1967 on the Muga river delta.

🚩 D2 🍴 A few restaurants and bars in the town (€–€€) 🚌 From Cadaqués, Figueres and Girona ❓ Market on Tue

PALAFRUGELL

This busy market town on the edge of the Lower Empordà plain has a down-to-earth Catalan atmosphere and several excellent beaches nearby. Once an important centre of cork production, the Museu del Suro (cork museum) displays the history of the cork industry, plus a selection of cork artefacts.

🚩 D4 🍴 Choice of restaurants and cafés (€–€€€) 🚌 From Girona and nearby beaches ❓ Market on Sun

PERALADA

The moated Renaissance castle that dominates this village now houses Catalonia's most stylish casino (► 81). Entrance to the castle museum, with its collections of glass and ceramics and the largest private library in Spain, also gives access to the 14th-century Carmelite convent within the castle walls. Some of the tours also include a tasting of cava from the castle cellars.

🚩 C1 Castle Museum: ☎ 972 53 81 25 🕐 Guided tours daily from 10am (closed Mon mid-Sep–Jun) 💰 Moderate

PERATALLADA

A bridge leads across the original moat to this medieval village (the name means 'hewn stone'), and the cobbled alleyways are full of stone houses bearing ancient coats of arms. People travel for long distances at weekends to eat in Peratallada's restaurants, and to wander the back streets around the 11th-century castle.

🚩 D4 🍴 Choice of restaurants and cafés (€–€€€)

TORROELLA DE MONTGRÍ

This delightful town of Gothic palaces, courtyards and narrow streets comes alive each Monday as the weekly market spills out in all directions from the porticoed main square, Plaça de la Vila. Stalls are piled high with local cheeses and sausages in this spot, where the *sardana*, the modern Catalan folk dance, was danced for the first time. The nearby Can Quintana cultural centre, housed in a historic mansion, contains the Museu de la Mediterrània, with interesting displays on local history, geology, wildlife and traditional music. A steep climb from the town centre leads to the restored Castell del Montgrí, built in 1294.

🚩 D3 🍴 Cafés and bars in the town centre (€) 🚌 From L'Estartit, Figueres, Girona and Palafrugell ❓ Market on Mon. Can Quintana: ✉ Carrer d'Ullà ☎ 972 75 51 80 🕐 Jul–Aug Mon–Sat 11–2, 6–9, Sun 11–2; Sep–Jun Mon, Wed–Sat 11–2, 5–8, Sun 11–2 💰 Free

SANTA PAU

The tourist capital of the Garrotxa region has at its heart a fortified medieval enclave with a well-restored baronial castle. The centre of the village is closed to traffic, so it is best to park outside and walk in through the original gateway, Portal Nou. Plaça Major, the main square, is as attractive as any in Catalonia, with wooden balconies, stone arcades and the Romanesque church of Santa Maria. The castle, first built in the 14th century, is in the neighbouring square, Placeta dels Balls. A short walk from here is the Mirador Portal del Mar, giving panoramic views over the Garrotxa valleys and a distant glimpse of the sea. Santa Pau is an excellent base for exploring this volcanic region – you can follow numerous well-marked footpaths, rent a mountain bike or a horse, take a ride in a horse-drawn carriage or fly over the volcanoes in a helicopter or a balloon.

🚩 B2 🍴 Choice of restaurants (€–€€) 🚌 Occasional buses from Banyoles and Olot ❓ For balloon flights contact Vol de Coloms ☎ 972 68 02 55

The castellated bell tower of Santa Maria church rises above the town of Santa Pau

Places to Have Lunch

ABRIL (€)
Healthy four-course lunch menu served at pleasant outdoor tables.
⊞ C4 ⊠ Carrer de Santa Clara 27, Girona ☎ 972 41 10 55

BOIRA (€–€€)
Tapas downstairs, as well as an upstairs restaurant with romantic views over the river.
⊞ C4 ⊠ Plaça Independència 17, Girona ☎ 972 21 96 05

CAP DE CREUS (€€)
Fish, salads and curries in a fabulous setting, ideal for watching the sun go down.
⊞ D1 ⊠ Cap de Creus ☎ 972 19 90 05

CAN SALVI (€€–€€€)
Fishy specialities on the seafront promenade.
⊞ D5 ⊠ Passeig del Mar 23, Sant Feliu de Guíxols ☎ 972 32 10 13

CURIA REIAL (€€)
Hearty meat dishes and 'volcanic cuisine' served on a terrace overlooking the medieval bridge.
⊞ B2 ⊠ Plaça Llibertat, Besalú ☎ 972 59 02 63

Take a break from the sun in a shaded restaurant

DURÁN (€€)
Top-notch Catalan cooking in Salvador Dalí's old haunt.
⊞ C2 ⊠ Carrer Lasauca 5, Figueres ☎ 972 50 12 50

EL PORT (€–€€€)
Fresh fish from the neighbouring market beneath the harbour walls. If you are looking for good value try the set lunch menu.
⊞ C6 ⊠ Esplanada del Port, Blanes ☎ 972 33 48 19

LA RIERA (€)
Hearty Catalan cooking at sensible prices in a village known for its food.
⊞ D4 ⊠ Plaça de les Voltes 3, Peratallada ☎ 972 63 41 42

SANTA MARTA (€€)
Attractive setting for this fish restaurant inside the Vila Vella.
⊞ C6 ⊠ Carrer Francesc Aromir 2, Tossa de Mar ☎ 972 34 04 72

TRAGAMAR (€€)
Stylish *tapas* and Catalan cuisine delightfully set right beside the beach.
⊞ D4 ⊠ Platja del Canadell, Calella de Palafrugell ☎ 972 61 51 89

COSTA BRAVA
where to...

Girona

ABRIL (€)

Fresh, light, healthy salads, meat and fish dishes and a good-value four-course lunchtime menu are served at this pretty little bistro, with tables on the square in summer.
✉ Carrer de Santa Clara 27
☎ 972 41 10 55 ⏰ Mon–Sat 8.30–8.30

L'ARCADA (€)

Tapas bar snacks downstairs, an Italian restaurant upstairs and tables outside on the Rambla.
✉ Rambla de la Llibertat 38
☎ 972 20 10 15
⏰ Daily 7am–1am

EL BALCÓ (€€)

This Argentinian restaurant is a paradise for serious meat-lovers, with beef, veal and duck grilled to perfection over an open fire.
✉ Carrer de les Hortes 16
☎ 972 22 31 61 ⏰ Lunch and dinner. Closed Sun

LE BISTROT (€)

Pancakes, salads and crusty bread pizzas at this popular old-style bistro, with tables outside on a pretty staircase in summer.
✉ Pujada Sant Domènec 4
☎ 972 21 88 03 ⏰ Lunch and dinner, daily

BLANC (€€)

Funky modern design and even funkier food – how about tuna with mango chutney followed by chocolate soup with olive oil?
✉ Carrer Nord 2
☎ 972 41 56 37
⏰ Lunch and dinner daily

BOIRA (€€)

Unusual *tapas* downstairs and a smart restaurant upstairs, featuring modern, light versions of traditional Catalan cuisine. Get here early for one of the tables overlooking the river.
✉ Plaça Independència 17
☎ 972 21 96 05 ⏰ Lunch and dinner, daily

CAFÉ MOZART (€€)

This popular restaurant serves delicious pizzas, cooked in a wood-fired oven, as well as fondues and grilled meat dishes; there is a wide range of salads.
✉ Plaça Independència 2
☎ 972 20 75 42 ⏰ Lunch and dinner. Closed Tue

CAL ROS (€€)

Traditional Catalan cooking with creative modern touches is the theme at this famous old town restaurant. Try the chocolate risotto with rice pudding ice-cream.
✉ Carrer Cort Reial 9 ☎ 972 21 91 76 ⏰ Lunch Tue–Sun, dinner Tue–Sat

CASA MARIETA (€€)

This popular old standby serves traditional Catalan food, such as seafood casserole and duck with pears, in agreeably old-fashioned surroundings on an arcaded square.
✉ Plaça Independència 5
☎ 972 20 10 16 ⏰ Lunch and dinner, Tue–Sun

CREPERIE BRETONNE (€€)

Delicious, authentic French pancakes and cider from Brittany served in fashionable and unusual surroundings.

✉ Carrer Cort Reial 14
☎ 972 21 81 20 🕐 Lunch and dinner, Tue–Sun

EL CUL DE LA LLEONA (€€)

An eclectic mix of Moroccan and Catalan cuisine – steamed aubergines, couscous, Arab pastries with mint tea.

✉ Carrer Calderers 8 ☎ 972 20 31 58 🕐 Lunch Tue–Sat, dinner Tue–Sun

DIVINUM (€)

This trendy student modern restaurant specialises in designer *tapas* such as foie gras with figs and sherry, plus plates of ham and cheese to share. The same owners have a wine bar on Carrer de l'Argenteria.

✉ Carrer General Fournàs 2
☎ 872 08 02 18 🕐 Mon–Sat 8am–11pm

LA LLIBRERIA (€)

A trendy student café attached to a radical bookshop, serving breakfasts, omelettes, snacks and good-value set meals.

✉ Carrer Ferreries Velles
☎ 972 20 48 18
🕐 Daily 9am–midnight

MAR PLAÇA (€€€)

This classy fish restaurant specialises in fish soups and casseroles and also serves delicious simply grilled fresh fish.

✉ Plaça Independència 3
☎ 972 20 59 62 🕐 Lunch Mon–Sat, dinner Tue–Sat

LA PENYORA (€€)

An intimate, arty restaurant in the old town,

serving creative market cuisine and a few Catalan staples.

✉ Carrer Nou del Teatre 3
☎ 972 21 89 48 🕐 Lunch and dinner. Closed Tue

EL POU DEL CALL (€€)

Come here for good-value Catalan cuisine with an excellent *menú del día*; located in the heart of the Jewish quarter, the Call Jueu.

✉ Carrer de la Força 14
☎ 972 22 37 74 🕐 Lunch and dinner. Closed Wed

LA RIBA (€€€)

La Riba is a fish restaurant and sushi bar with windows overlooking the river.

✉ Plaça Independència 12
☎ 872 08 14 90 🕐 Lunch and dinner, daily

LA TAVERNA (€)

Tapas, omelettes, local sausages and cheeses, as well as home-made pâtés and Basque cider, are the favourites here, all served at outdoor tables in the pleasant setting of a new town square.

✉ Plaça Santa Susanna 2
☎ 972 21 13 81
🕐 Open all day, Mon–Sat

ZANPANZAR (€)

A Basque-style *tapas* bar where the *pintxos* (bite-sized open sandwiches) are laid out along the counter. You help yourself and then add up the cocktail sticks on your plate in order to settle your bill. Basque cider is a speciality.

✉ Carrer Cort Reial 12
☎ 972 21 28 43
🕐 Lunch and dinner, Tue–Sun

OPENING TIMES

The Spanish like to eat late – typically between 1 and 3 at lunchtime and any time after 9 in the evening. If you get hungry before these times, *tapas* bars are usually open all day. Most restaurants close for one day a week and many have an annual holiday or reduce their hours in winter, so it is always a good idea to telephone in advance.

Central Costa Brava

SET MENUS

Most restaurants offer a *menú del día* at lunchtime, and some in the evening, too – a set-price three-course meal, with mineral water or wine included. You may not get much choice (typically two or three options for each course), but what you do get will invariably be cheap, filling and freshly cooked. A full meal, with drinks, will usually cost about the same as a main course from the *carta*.

BEGUR

EL BODEGÓN (€€€)

Fresh local fish is roasted in a wood-burning oven at this back-street restaurant in the old centre of town.
✉ Carrer Pi i Ralló ☎ 972 62 20 13 ⏰ Lunch and dinner, Tue–Sun

BESALÚ

CA'N QUEI (€)

A good-value bar serving snacks, sandwiches, salads and hot meals.
✉ Plaça Sant Vincenç ☎ 972 59 00 85 ⏰ Lunch and dinner, Thu–Tue

CURIA REIAL (€€)

This restaurant in the 14th-century Royal Court building specialises in Catalan meat and game dishes. There is a terrace overlooking the river and the medieval bridge.
✉ Plaça Llibertat ☎ 972 59 02 63 ⏰ Lunch and dinner. Closed Tue

ELS FOGONS DE CAN LLAUDES (€€€)

This elegant restaurant is housed in a Romanesque chapel facing the church of Sant Pere. The emphasis is on meat and game dishes. Booking essential.
✉ Prat de Sant Pere 6 ☎ 972 59 08 58 ⏰ Lunch and dinner. Closed Tue

CALELLA DE PALAFRUGELL

CAN PALET (€€)

Small, attractive seafood restaurant with tables beside Calau beach.
✉ Carrer Calau 8 ☎ 972 61 45 45 ⏰ Lunch and dinner, daily

TRAGAMAR (€€)

Seaside branch of a popular Barcelona restaurant chain, offering designer *tapas* and sophisticated Catalan cuisine in informal, stylish surroundings on the beachside promenade. In summer, children run in and out while their parents eat.
✉ Platja del Canadell ☎ 972 61 51 89 ⏰ Lunch and dinner, daily. Closed Tue in winter

L'ESTARTIT

LA GAVIOTA (€€€)

Seafood restaurant at the end of the promenade with a good view of the Medes Islands. Among the unusual specialities are red mullet with rosemary, and angler-fish in sea-urchin sauce.
✉ Passeig Marítim 92 ☎ 972 75 20 19 ⏰ Lunch and dinner Tue–Sun

OLOT

LA DEU (€€)

The famous Garrotxa potato dish *patates de la Deu* was invented at this traditional Catalan restaurant, which offers hearty 'volcanic cooking' in a country house on the edge of town.
✉ Carretera La Deu ☎ 972 26 10 04 ⏰ Lunch daily, dinner Mon–Sat

LES COLES (€€€)

Michelin-star restaurant in a 13th-century farmhouse, with striking avant-garde design. Lovely ambience for fine food.
✉ Carretera de la Canya ☎ 972 26 92 09 ⏰ Lunch Tue–Sat, dinner Wed–Sat

PALAFRUGELL

LA XICRA (€€€)

Classic Empordan cooking in a village house. Specials include seafood casserole and chickpeas with baby octopus and ham.

✉ Carrer de Sant Antoni 17 ☎ 972 30 56 30 🕔 Lunch Thu–Tue, dinner Thu–Mon

PALS

MAS DE TORRENT (€€€)

Innovative meat and fish dishes prepared with typical Catalan flair, in a beautiful 18th-century farmhouse.

✉ Torrent, between Pals and Palafrugell ☎ 902 55 03 21 🕔 Lunch and dinner daily

PERATALLADA

CAN BONAY (€€)

A third-generation family restaurant offering Catalan classics such as goose with turnips.

✉ Plaça de les Voltes 13 ☎ 972 63 40 34 🕔 Lunch and dinner, Tue–Sun

CAN NAU (€€)

Hearty Catalan casseroles of snails, rabbit or chicken, served in the ground floor of a village home.

✉ Plaça Esquiladors 2 ☎ 972 63 40 35 🕔 Lunch and dinner, daily

LA PAÏSSA D'EN CARDINA (€€)

Funky bistro offering pizzas, pasta, salads and grilled meat in a back-street house with a summer terrace.

✉ Carrer Jaume II 10 ☎ 972 63 47 08 🕔 Lunch and dinner, daily

LA RIERA (€€)

Simple Catalan cooking – grilled meat, sausages, snails – at this hotel with a delightful summer terrace on the main square.

✉ Plaça de les Voltes 3 ☎ 972 63 41 42 🕔 Lunch and dinner. Closed Tue in winter

PÚBOL

CAN BOSCH (€)

Traditional village restaurant serving hearty portions and a good-value set lunch.

✉ Beside the castle ☎ 972 48 83 57 🕔 Lunch daily, dinner Fri–Sun

SANT JOAN DE LES ABADESSES

CASA RUDES (€)

Home-cooked Catalan favourites and an old-style grocery shop.

✉ Carrer de Sant Antoni 17 ☎ 972 30 56 30 🕔 Lunch Thu–Tue, dinner Thu–Mon

SANTA PAU

CAN SASTRE (€€)

The place to try Garrotxa cuisine featuring local sausages, mushrooms and beans, located in a delightful square.

✉ Placeta dels Balls 6 ☎ 972 68 04 21 🕔 Lunch Tue–Sun, dinner Tue–Sat

TAMARIU

ES DOFI (€€)

One of the best of the many fish restaurants that stretch along the seafront promenade.

✉ Passeig del Mar 22 ☎ 972 62 00 43 🕔 Lunch and dinner, daily

TAPAS

Tapas are a Spanish institution. Originally a free 'lid' (*tapa*) of ham placed across a drink, nowadays they consist of small portions of everything from octopus to olives. Locals tend to snack on *tapas* during the day before going home for dinner, but several portions can make a filling meal in itself. Popular *tapas* include stuffed peppers, fried squid rings and plates of cured ham. And you don't have to look at a menu – just point to what you want in the cabinet beneath the bar.

The North Coast & Beyond

VEGETARIANS

Vegetarians could have a hard time in the Costa Brava – unless they are prepared to eat fish. *Tapas* bars usually have vegetarian options, including a range of omelettes; or you could have a plate of *pa amb tomàquet* (bread rubbed with tomato) accompanied by a large Catalan salad without the meat. Unfortunately, many vegetable dishes include small pieces of meat or fish, but you can always try asking for it *sense carn* (without meat).

CADAQUÉS

CAN PELAYO (€€)
Small, family-run fish restaurant behind the harbour serving grilled fish, paella and seafood casserole.
✉ Carrer Pruna 11 ☎ 972 25 83 56 ⏰ Lunch and dinner, Thu–Tue

CASA ANITA (€€)
At Casa Anita the simple, rustic home cooking is served at communal wooden tables. The authentic atmosphere is a popular choice for locals and tourists alike.
✉ Carrer Miquel Rosset 16 ☎ 972 25 84 71 ⏰ Lunch and dinner, Tue–Sun

LA SIRENA (€€)
Fresh fish and vegetarian choices in this intimate restaurant, hidden away in the back streets of the Jewish quarter around the church.
✉ Carrer d'es Call ☎ 972 25 89 74 ⏰ Lunch and dinner, Wed–Sun

CAP DE CREUS

CAP DE CREUS (€€)
This English-run bar beside the lighthouse offers curries, salads, tapas and fresh fish dishes. The panoramic terrace is great for a sunset drink.
✉ Cap de Creus ☎ 972 19 90 05 ⏰ Daily 10am–1am in summer, Mon–Thu 12–8, Fri–Sun 11–11 in winter

EMPÚRIES

MESÓN DEL CONDE (€€)
The best of the restaurants in the village of Sant Martí d'Empúries is just a short walk from the ruins. In spring try the grilled *calçots*, a local onion served with *romesco* (tomato, onion and pepper) sauce.
✉ Plaça Major, Sant Martí d'Empúries ☎ 972 77 03 06 ⏰ Lunch and dinner daily in summer, closed Mon eve and Tue in winter

L'ESCALA

ELS PESCADORS (€€€)
Traditional Catalan cooking using top-quality local ingredients – grilled fish, fresh seafood and *sarsuela* fish casserole.
✉ Carrer Port d'en Perris 3 ☎ 972 77 07 28 ⏰ Lunch and dinner, daily. Closed Nov and Sun eve in winter

FIGUERES

ANTAVIANA (€€)
Stylish Catalan and French cuisine with an emphasis on duck – try the carpaccio of duck breast or the beef in Cabrales (blue cheese) sauce.
✉ Carrer Llers 5 ☎ 972 51 03 77 ⏰ Lunch and dinner, Wed–Sun

CAFÉ HOTEL PARIS (€)
This pavement café on the promenade makes a great spot for lunch, serving sandwiches, snacks, pizzas and a good-value *menú del día*.
✉ Rambla 10 ☎ 972 50 07 13 ⏰ 8am–11pm daily

DALÍCATESSEN (€)
This trendy sandwich and salad bar is a good place for a snack before or after a visit to the Dalí museum.

✉ Carrer Sant Pere 19 ☎ 972
51 11 93 ⏰ 8am–9pm daily

EL DRAGÓN DORADO
(€)
If you tire of Spanish and
Catalan cuisine, try this
Chinese restaurant near
the Dalí museum, which
proves a popular choice
for locals and visitors.
✉ Pujada del Castell 9
☎ 972 54 00 17
⏰ Lunch and dinner, daily

DURÁN (€€)
Salvador Dalí's favourite
hangout is still full of
character, and continues
to serve good local food
served in a traditional
Catalan style.
✉ Carrer Lasauca 5
☎ 972 50 12 50
⏰ Lunch and dinner, daily

EMPORDÀ (€€€)
This famous hotel, just
outside Figueres on the
old road to France, has a
magnificent garden
terrace, where traditional
Empordan cooking is
served up with modern
flair. The former chef
here, Josep Mercader,
is considered to be
the founder of modern
Catalan cuisine.
✉ Antiga Carretera de França
☎ 972 50 05 62 ⏰ Lunch
and dinner, daily

EL SETRILL D'OR (€)
For good pizzas and fresh
pasta dishes, and an
excellent-value set lunch.
The comfortable
furnishings and oil
paintings on the walls add
to the atmosphere.
✉ Carrer Tortellà 12
☎ 972 50 55 40
⏰ Lunch and dinner, Wed–Sun

LLANÇÀ

LA BRASA (€€)
Local squid and
anchovies, seafood
casserole and charcoal-
grilled meat, served on a
pretty terrace just back
from the harbour.
✉ Plaça Catalunya 6 ☎ 972
38 02 02 ⏰ Lunch and dinner
Jul–Aug daily. Closed Sep–Jun
Mon eve and Tue

PERALADA

MAS MOLI (€€€)
Roast lamb and suckling
pig, cooked in an old-style
wood oven, and housed in
the setting of an old mill.
✉ Carretera Antiga de
Vilabertran ☎ 972 53 82 81
⏰ Lunch Tue–Sun, dinner
Tue–Sat

PORTLLIGAT

CHEZ PIERRE (€€)
Intimate, stylish bistro
offering French and
Catalan cuisine with a hint
of oriental influence.
✉ Carrer Miquel Rosset 48
☎ 972 25 84 16 ⏰ Dinner
only, Wed–Mon

ROSES

EL BULLI (€€€)
Quite simply one of the
finest restaurants in Spain
(► panel). Book ahead.
✉ Cala Montjoi ☎ 972 15 04
57 ⏰ Dinner only, Apr–Jun
Wed–Sun; Jul–Sep daily

FLOR DE LIS (€€€)
Sophisticated French and
seafood cuisine in a pretty
cottage in the back streets.
✉ Carrer Coscanilles 47
☎ 972 25 43 16 ⏰ Dinner
only, Wed–Mon, Easter–Oct

EL BULLI

Food-lovers make the
pilgrimage from all over
France and Spain to eat at this
famous restaurant, in an
exceptional setting looking
down over a tranquil cove.
The chef, Ferran Adrià, has
gained three Michelin stars for
his highly personal inter-
pretations of Catalan cuisine.
His sci-fi approach to cooking
has even seen him open a
laboratory in Barcelona, and
his style has been imitated
with varying degrees of
success by most of the new
generation of Catalan chefs. A
meal at El Bulli is a once-in-a-
lifetime experience, and you
should plan accordingly –
budget for at least €200 per
person and book several
months in advance. If you
really want to do it in style,
arrive by yacht.

The South Coast & Beyond

WINE

Catalonia produces some excellent wines, but the best wines on the menu will probably come from La Rioja. Riojan reds, made with the *tempranillo* grape, are superb. Those labelled *crianza* are aged in oak; *reserva* and *gran reserva* have been aged for longer. Don't forget *cava*, Catalan sparkling wine, which is such good value that you don't even need a special excuse to drink it.

BLANES

EL PORT (€€)

Come here to eat freshly caught fish beneath the harbour walls. The lobster and sea bass are expensive, but there is a very affordable set lunch, which features paella, mussels and fresh fish.

✉ Esplanada del Port
☎ 972 33 48 19
🕓 Lunch and dinner, daily

EL VENTALL (€€€)

One of the top restaurants in this area is found in a country house between Blanes and Lloret de Mar. The cooking is Mediterranean and modern Catalan, and in summer you can eat outside on a garden terrace.

✉ Carretera de Lloret km2
☎ 972 33 29 81 🕓 Lunch and dinner, Wed–Mon

LLORET DE MAR

LES PETXINES (€€€)

New-wave chef Paula Casanovas turns out inventive Catalan-Mediterranean cooking in a surprising venue on the beachfront at Lloret de Mar. If you don't want to splash out, have a salad on the summer terrace.

✉ Passeig Jacint Verdaguer 16
☎ 972 36 41 37 🕓 Lunch and dinner, daily

EL TRULL (€€€)

This popular fish restaurant overlooking a pretty cove has a terrace with a pool in summer. Choose your own lobster then watch it being grilled.

✉ Cala Canyelles
☎ 972 36 49 28
🕓 Lunch and dinner, daily

PALAMÓS

LA GAMBA (€€€)

The best local seafood, simply prepared, on a terrace overlooking the harbour. Specialities are prawns, *suquet* casserole, (white fish and potatoes poached in white wine), oven-baked fish and stuffed sea urchins.

✉ Plaça Sant Pere 1 ☎ 972 31 46 33 🕓 Lunch and dinner, Thu–Tue

MARIA DE CADAQUÉS (€€€)

Trendy fish restaurant which displays paintings by local artists on the walls. Fish comes fresh from the local fleet to become delicious *suquets*.

✉ Carrer Tauler i Servià 6
☎ 972 31 40 09 🕓 Lunch Tue–Sun, dinner Tue–Sat

PLATJA D'ARO

EL CAU DEL PERNIL (€€)

This traditional cellar-bar specialises in ham, as well as several varieties of sausages and charcoal-grilled meat. A meat eater's heaven.

✉ Avinguda Sant Feliu 7
☎ 972 81 72 09 🕓 Lunch and dinner, daily

FANALS PLATJA (€€–€€€)

Seafood restaurant looking out on to the beach. The specialities, including lobster paella, are expensive, but there are more modestly priced

delights on the menu.
✉ Passeig Marítim 92
☎ 972 81 98 26 ◐ Lunch
and dinner, daily Apr–Oct, lunch
only in winter

SANT FELIU DE GUÍXOLS

BAHÍA (€€)
Popular fish restaurant on
the promenade. Start with
a pica-pica, a selection of a
dozen fishy *tapas*.
✉ Passeig del Mar 17
☎ 972 32 02 19 ◐ Lunch
and dinner, daily

CAN SALVI (€€)
The emphasis here is on
locally caught fish,
including anchovies,
salmon and sole in
Roquefort sauce.
✉ Passeig del Mar 23
☎ 972 32 10 13 ◐ Lunch
and dinner. Closed Thu

EL DORADO MAR (€€)
What better than fresh
seafood served on a
terrace overlooking the
sea.
✉ Passeig Marítim President Irla
15 ☎ 972 32 62 86 ◐ Lunch
and dinner, daily

TOSSA DE MAR

**LA CUINA DE CAN
SIMÓN (€€€)**
Michelin-star restaurant in
an old cottage near the
town walls.
✉ Carrerer Portal 24 ☎ 972
34 12 69 ◐ Lunch Wed–Sun,
dinner Wed–Sat (open daily in
summer)

SANTA MARTA (€€)
Pretty terrace restaurant in
the heart of the Vila Vella,
specialising in fish dishes,
including *cim-i-tomba*, a

monkfish, potato and
garlic casserole.
✉ Carrer Francesc Aromir 2
☎ 972 34 04 72
◐ Easter–Sep, lunch and dinner
Thu–Tue

VIC

ÁGAPE (€€)
Hip bookshop-café
offering vegetarian and fish
dishes and world cuisines.
Near the Roman temple.
✉ Carrer Progrés 2 ☎ 938 89
26 46 ◐ Mon–Sat 9–6

BASSET (€€)
Arty restaurant featuring
modern variations on
traditional Catalan cuisine.
✉ Carrer Sant Sadurní 4
☎ 938 89 02 12 ◐ Lunch and
dinner, Mon–Sat

CAFÉ NOU (€)
Noisy, bustling locals'
pub, packed out on
market days. The set
menu here is one of the
best deals anywhere.
✉ Plaça Major 23 ☎ 938 86
25 02 ◐ Lunch and dinner,
Tue–Sun

EL JARDINET (€€)
Catalan cooking with a
hint of French in a
delightful restaurant in
the back streets of the
old town.
✉ Carrer dels Corretgers 8
☎ 938 86 28 77 ◐ Lunch
Tue–Sun, dinner Tue–Sat

LA TAULA (€€)
Old mansion in the
medieval centre with good
choice of *tapas* and main
meals. Salt cod dishes are
a particular speciality.
✉ Plaça Don Miquel de Clariana
4 ☎ 938 86 32 29 ◐ Lunch
Tue–Sun, dinner Tue–Sat

COFFEE

In Spain, *un café* after your
meal means only one thing –
café solo (*café sol* in Catalan),
which is short, strong and
black, like an espresso. If you
want hot milk added, ask for
café con leche or *café amb
llet*. If the waiter brings you a
brandy or a liqueur with your
coffee, this is a treat on the
house. Drink up and enjoy!

Girona & Central Costa Brava

AIGUABLAVA

AIGUA BLAVA (€€€)

One of the gems of the Catalan coast, with white-painted buildings tumbling down towards a rocky cove. Many rooms are in villas in the gardens; also has tennis courts and a pool.

✉ Platja de Fornells ☎ 972 62 20 58; www.aiguablava.com ⏰ Mar–Oct

PARADOR DE AIGUABLAVA (€€€)

A member of the state-run chain of *paradors*, set amid delightful pine groves. Steps down to the beach and good views of the bay.

✉ Platja d'Aiguablava ☎ 972 62 21 62; www.parador.es ⏰ All year

BEGUR

ROSA (€)

Family-run hotel in the heart of town. Bike rental available.

✉ Carrer Pi i Ralló 11 ☎ 972 62 30 15; www.hotel-rosa.com ⏰ Mar–Nov

BESALÚ

ELS JARDINS DE LA MARTANA (€€)

Boutique hotel in a town house beside the medieval bridge; gardens overlooking the river.

✉ Carrer del Pont 2 ☎ 972 59 00 09; www.lamartana.com ⏰ All year

COMTE TALLAFERRO (€€)

Stylish, comfortable rooms in a 16th-century town house overlooking the main square. An added bonus is that guests can use the swimming pool at Fonda Siqués, a traditional coaching inn and restaurant run by the same family.

✉ Carrer Ganganell 2 ☎ 972 59 16 09; www.grupcalparent.com ⏰ All year

MARIA (€)

Simple rooms around the courtyard of a 16th-century building on the central square.

✉ Plaça Llibertat 15 ☎ 972 59 01 06 ⏰ All year

LA BISBAL

CASTELL D'EMPORDÁ (€€€)

Luxury hotel set in a 12th-century castle, with a pool in the extensive gardens and rooms filled with art and antiques.

✉ Castell d'Empordà ☎ 972 64 62 54; www.castelldemporda.com ⏰ Mar–Oct

CALELLA DE PALAFRUGELL

SANT ROC (€€)

Traditional seaside hotel in a spectacular position on a rocky outcrop looking down over the bay. Steps lead from the hotel to the beach.

✉ Plaça de l'Atlàntic 2 ☎ 972 61 42 50; www.santroc.com ⏰ Apr–Oct

LA TORRE (€€)

Simple hotel with a terrace overlooking the bay between Calella and Llafranc.

✉ Passeig de la Torre 28 ☎ 972 61 46 03; www.hotel-latorre.com ⏰ Apr–Sep

GIRONA

BELLMIRALL (€)
This medieval stone mansion, in the old town, has been turned into a charming hostel with simple but comfortable rooms overlooking the cathedral.
✉ Carrer Bellmirall 3
☎ 972 20 40 09
🕒 Mar–Dec

CIUTAT DE GIRONA (€€)
Cool, minimalist design hotel nicely located close to the old town and the river.
✉ Carrer Nord 2
☎ 972 48 30 38; www.hotel-ciutatdegirona.com 🕒 All year

HISTÒRIC (€€)
Stylish modern hotel and self-catering apartments in a beautifully restored building near the cathedral.
✉ Carrer Bellmirall 4A
☎ 972 22 35 83;
www.hotelhistoric.com
🕒 All year

PENINSULA (€€)
Comfortable hotel in an excellent central location, beside the Pont de Pedra and close to Girona's old town quarter.
✉ Carrer Nou 3 ☎ 972 20 38 00; www.novarahotels.com 🕒 All year

LLAFRANC

EL FAR (€€€)
Just nine rooms set around an interior courtyard in an old chapel, high on the cliffs. Some of the rooms have magnificent sea views.
✉ Cap de Sant Sebastià
☎ 972 30 16 39; www.elfar.net
🕒 Feb–Dec

LLAFRANCH (€€)
Stylish, comfortable hotel on the seafront promenade, with a reputation for good food. One of the first tourist hotels on the Costa Brava, still run by the same family. Salvador Dalí was a regular visitor; the bar is lined with pictures of him with flamenco performers and the brothers who ran the hotel.
✉ Passeig de Cipsela 16
☎ 972 30 02 08;
www.hllafranch.com 🕒 All year

PALS

MAS DE TORRENT (€€€)
An 18th-century farmhouse, with period furniture, contemporary Catalan art and flower-filled gardens. Known for its innovative Catalan cuisine.
✉ Torrent, between Pals and Palafrugell ☎ 902 55 03 21; www.mastorrent.com 🕒 All year

PERATALLADA

HOSTAL BLAU (€€)
Offbeat, arty hotel with six rooms in an 18th-century town house.
✉ Carrer Forn 2 ☎ 972 63 41 85; www.hostalblau.com
🕒 All year

TAMARIU

TAMARIU (€€)
A small and friendly hotel right beside the beach.
✉ Passeig del Mar 2 ☎ 972 62 00 31; www.tamariu.com
🕒 Mar–Oct

HOTELS, *PENSIONS* AND *PARADORS*

All tourist accommodation in Catalonia is strictly classified and graded by the government. Hotels are graded from one to five stars according to facilities; *pensions*, with fewer facilities but sometimes just as comfortable, are graded either one or two. *Pensions* will not necessarily offer rooms with private bathrooms. *Paradors* are luxury, state-run hotels, mostly in historic buildings or areas of scenic beauty. The only two *paradors* in the Costa Brava region are at Aiguablava and Vic.

71

The North Coast & Beyond

APARTMENTS

A week in a self-catering apartment or villa can work out a lot cheaper than staying in a hotel. Most can only be booked through tour operators, but a few are advertised individually by their owners or available for rent through local agencies in the Costa Brava. Some apartments have their own private pools. If you want an apartment in summer it is essential to book several months in advance.

CADAQUÉS

LLANÉ PETIT (€€)

Beachside hotel on the southern side of the bay, a short walk from the town centre. On the way into town you pass Port Alguer, a scene from a Dalí painting which has hardly changed since he captured it in 1924.

✉ Carrer Dr Bartomeus 37
☎ 972 25 10 20;
www.llanepetit.com
🕐 Mar–Dec

PLAYA SOL (€€)

Old-fashioned seaside hotel with a swimming pool in the gardens and a small beach decked out with fishing boats directly opposite.

✉ Platja Pianc 3 ☎ 972 25 81 00; www.playasol.com
🕐 Mar–Oct

LA RESIDÈNCIA (€€)

Stylish Modernista hotel on the seafront, with a sundial by Dalí and an art gallery.

✉ Carrer Caritat Serinyana 1
☎ 972 25 83 12 ;
www.laresidencia.net
🕐 All year

ROCAMAR (€€)

Traditional seaside hotel with a sea-water pool and steps down to a rocky cove.

✉ Carrer Dr Bartomeus
☎ 972 25 81 50;
www.rocamar.com 🕐 All year

CASTELLÓ D'EMPÚRIES

CANET (€€)

Delightful town-centre hotel with a swimming pool in its interior courtyard.

✉ Plaça Joc de la Pilota 2
☎ 972 25 03 40;
www.hotelcanet.com
🕐 Mar–Oct

HOTEL DE LA MONEDA (€€)

This four-star hotel opened in 2002 in a restored 17th-century mansion in the old Jewish quarter. Facilities include a pool and free internet access.

✉ Plaça de la Moneda 8
☎ 972 15 86 02;
www.hoteldelamoneda.com
🕐 Mar–Nov

PALAU MACELLI (€€)

Stay in a restored 17th-century Italian palace near the cathedral. Carriage rides are available, and dinner is served in the garden in summer.

✉ Carrer Carbonar 1 ☎ 972 25 05 67; www.palaumacelli.com
🕐 All year

EMPÚRIES

HOSTAL EMPÚRIES (€€)

Try this newly refurbished old-style beach hotel near the Greek and Roman ruins.

✉ Platja de Portitxol
☎ 972 77 02 07;
www.hostalempuries.com
🕐 All year

FIGUERES

BON RETORN (€€)

This modern hotel on the outskirts of town avoids the problems of parking in the centre. There is a swimming pool in the gardens.

✉ Carretera N11 ☎ 972 50 46 23; www.bonretorn.com
🕐 All year

DURÁN (€€)

An atmospheric, old-world hotel in the centre of town, where Salvador Dalí used to meet his friends for lunch. It also has one of the finest restaurants in Figueres.

✉ Carrer Lasauca 5 ☎ 972 50 12 50; www.hotelduran.com
🕐 All year

EMPORDÀ (€€)

This stylish hotel was the birthplace of the new Catalan cuisine and is still an essential place of pilgrimage for food-lovers.
✉ Antiga Carretera de França (N11) ☎ 972 50 05 62; www.hotelemporda.com
🕐 All year

RAMBA (€€)

Small, stylish, two-star hotel in a 19th-century town house on the Rambla.
✉ Rambla 33 ☎ 972 67 60 02; www.hotelrambla.net
🕐 All year

PERALADA

GOLF PERALADA (€€€)

Five-star golf and spa resort located at the centre of the golf course. Among the facilities is a vinotherapy wine spa.
✉ Carrer Rocabertí ☎ 972 53 88 30; www.golfperalada.com
🕐 All year

EL PORT DE LA SELVA

PORTO CRISTO (€)

A comfortable, three-star hotel, set just back from the beach in a restored 19th-century house.
✉ Carrer Major 69 ☎ 972 38 70 62; www.hotelportocristo.com
🕐 Mar–Oct

PORTLLIGAT

CALINA (€€)

This apartment-style hotel, close to the beach, has a series of self-catering apartments set around a swimming pool.
✉ Portlligat ☎ 972 25 88 51; www.hotelcalina.com
🕐 Mar–Oct

PORTLLIGAT (€€)

A peaceful, two-star hotel with a children's playground, a swimming pool and views over Dalí's waterside house and out to sea.
✉ Portlligat ☎ 972 25 81 62 🕐 All year

ROSES

ALMADRABA PARK (€€€)

Four-star hotel with modern facilities, on a rocky cliff overlooking the cove of Almadrava.
✉ Platja de Almadrava ☎ 972 25 65 50; www.almadrabapark.com
🕐 Apr–Oct

HOSTAL DEL SOL (€)

Cosy, family-run beach hostel with works by local artists on the walls.
✉ Avinguda del Rhode 42 ☎ 972 25 60 37 🕐 Apr–Sep

VISTABELLA (€€€)

This five-star hotel, beside the beach at Canyelles, has its own landing-stage for boats and offers spa-like treatments ranging from massage to Turkish baths.
✉ Cala Canyelles Petites ☎ 972 25 62 00; www.vistabellahotel.com
🕐 May–Sep

AGROTOURISM

A number of farmers in the region let out rooms in their houses or in restored farm buildings on their land, on a self-catering, bed-and-breakfast or full-board basis. This can be a great way of getting to meet a local family and enjoying an active holiday away from the beach resorts. A brochure on rural tourism in the Costa Brava is available from Turisme Rural Girona ☎ 972 22 60 15, or www.gironarural.org

The South Coast & Beyond

SPA HOTELS

The waters of the Selva region, south of Girona, have long been known for their healing properties. Caldes de Malavella, a Roman spa town, has two elegant spa hotels, built around the turn of the 20th century in neoclassical and Modernist styles: Balneari Prats ☎ 972 47 00 51, www.balneariprats.com, and Vichy Catalán ☎ 972 47 00 00, www.balnearivichycatalan.com. Termes Orión ☎ 972 84 00 65 is another spa-hotel in the nearby town of Santa Coloma de Farners. In 2002 it opened the Magma spa centre, which offers a wide range of therapies to day visitors. (Closed Tue.)

CALONGE

PARK HOTEL SAN JORGE (€€€)
Four-star hotel overlooking a rugged stretch of coastline, with access on foot to a pair of secluded coves.
✉ Carretera de Palamós
☎ 972 65 23 11; www.silken-parksanjorge.com ◉ All year

LLORET DE MAR

GRAN HOTEL MONTERREY (€€)
Luxury hotel on the outskirts of the resort, with a pool and tennis courts in extensive grounds.
✉ Carretera Blanes-Tossa de Mar ☎ 972 34 60 54; www.ghmonterrey.com
◉ Apr–Oct

SANTA MARTA (€€€)
Smart, modern hotel set in a pine wood behind the quiet cove of Santa Cristina, with large flower gardens and stunning sea views.
✉ Platja Santa Cristina
☎ 972 36 49 04; www.hotelstamarta.com
◉ Feb–Nov

PALAMÓS

LA FOSCA (€€)
Modest but comfortable two-star pension, set back from the beach in its own quiet bay.
✉ Passeig de la Fosca 24
☎ 972 60 10 71 ◉ All year

LA MALCONTENTA (€€€)
This beautifully restored farmhouse is now a luxury country house hotel with a pool in the gardens.
✉ Platja de Castell 12
☎ 972 31 23 30; www.lamalcontentahotel.com
◉ All year

TRIAS (€€)
Luxury and elegance go hand in hand in this modern beach hotel, with a range of facilities including a swimming pool and solarium.
✉ Passeig del Mar ☎ 972 60 18 00; www.hoteltrias.com
◉ All year

PLATJA D'ARO

PLATJA PARK (€€)
Busy, four-star hotel in the centre of town, with a children's pool and play area and a programme of nightly entertainment. The beach is about 10 minutes' walk away.
✉ Avinguda de Strasburg 10
☎ 972 81 68 05
◉ Apr–Oct

XALOC (€€)
A comfortable, three-star hotel, with a quiet terrace garden leading to the small beach of Platja Rovira.
✉ Cala Rovira ☎ 972 81 73 00 ◉ May–Sep

S'AGARÓ

HOSTAL DE LA GAVINA (€€€)
The most famous hotel on the Costa Brava was opened in 1924 and designed by the Catalan Modernist architect Rafael Masó in the style of a Gothic villa. Film stars such as Orson Welles and Elizabeth Taylor have stayed here, enjoying its antiques, tapestries and marble floors, its fine

Catalan cuisine and its landscaped gardens on a rocky promontory above the sea.

✉ Plaça de la Rosaleda
☎ 972 32 11 00;
www.lagavina.com ⏲ Apr–Oct

S'AGARÓ (€€)

Less exclusive than its famous neighbour, this luxury four-star hotel also has its own extensive gardens, just a short walk from the beach.

✉ Platja Sant Pol ☎ 972 32 52 00; www.hotelsagaro.com
⏲ All year

S'AGARÓ MAR (€€)

A lovely family hotel with pool, playground and terrace gardens in the pine woods above Sant Pol beach, near S'Agaró.

✉ Camí de la Caleta ☎ 972 32 11 40 ⏲ Apr–Oct

SANT FELIU DE GUÍXOLS

PLAÇA (€€)

Comfortable three-star hotel with balconies overlooking the market square, a short way back from the beach.

✉ Plaça Mercat 22 ☎ 972 32 51 55; www.hotelplaza.org
⏲ All year

TOSSA DE MAR

DIANA (€€)

Attractive seafront villa, built in the Modernist style, with arched windows, stained glass and featuring a fireplace by Antoni Gaudí in the lounge.

✉ Plaça d'Espanya 6 ☎ 972 34 18 86; www.diana-hotel.com
⏲ Apr–Oct

GRAN HOTEL REYMAR (€€€)

Arguably the smartest hotel in Tossa, with a heated swimming pool and tennis courts and a pleasant garden with lovely views looking down over the Mar Menuda beach.

✉ Platja Mar Menuda ☎ 972 34 03 12; www.ghreymar.com
⏲ May–Oct

MAR MENUDA (€€)

Peaceful, traditional hotel on the beach of the same name, just around the bay from Tossa's main beach promenade.

✉ Platja Mar Menuda
☎ 972 34 10 00;
www.hotelmarmenuda.com
⏲ May–Oct

VIC

CIUTAT DE VIC (€€)

The best choice in town – a smart, modern business hotel on the edge of the historic centre.

✉ Passatge Can Mastrot
☎ 938 89 25 51; www.nh-hotels.com ⏲ All year

PARADOR DE VIC (€€)

This state-run inn was designed in Catalan farmhouse style, and set in a pine grove overlooking a reservoir at the foot of the Montseny mountains. The restaurant serves up hearty Catalan stews and fresh angler-fish with garlic mayonnaise. There are wonderful views of the mountains from the outdoor swimming pool.

✉ Pantà de Sau, Carrer de Roda de Ter (14km from Vic) ☎ 938 12 23 23; www.parador.es
⏲ All year

CAMPING

The Costa Brava has over 100 official campsites, most of them clustered around the large coastal resorts. Many are situated right beside beaches, and nearly all have swimming pools. Campsites are classified as first, second or third class, according to facilities. An annual guide, available in local bookshops, lists all the campsites; information is also available from local tourist offices. Relax-Naturista is an official nudist campsite near Palafrugell. For information call ☎ 972 30 08 18.

Markets

MERCAT DEL RAM

One of Catalonia's biggest markets takes place in Vic a week before Easter. What began as a livestock fair has grown into a celebration of all things Catalan, with *sardana* dancing and the election of a palm queen. Farmers still come to the market to trade cattle and poultry, and stalls sell decorated palm fronds which are given as Easter presents. The fair takes place on the Saturday immediately preceding Palm Sunday.

GIRONA

MERCAT MUNICIPAL

This indoor market near the Plaça de Catalunya has stalls selling a wide range of meat, fish and cheeses, fresh fruit and vegetables, and ready-prepared meals. A good place to stock up on provisions for a picnic. On Saturdays there are also outdoor produce markets in the square.

✉ Plaça Salvador Espriu
🕐 Mon–Sat 7–1.30

MERCAT SEMANAL

Girona's weekly markets take place on Tuesday and Saturday, on the edge of Parc de la Devesa. On Saturdays a colourful flower market is set up on the Rambla, along with arts and crafts stalls on Pont de Pedra.

✉ Passeig de la Devesa
🕐 Tue, Sat all year

WEEKLY MARKETS

Market day in any of the Costa Brava's towns is the best place to meet the locals and soak up the atmosphere of small-town Catalonia. The usual pattern is for fresh fruit, vegetables and flowers to be sold in or around the main square, together with specialist stalls selling meats and cheeses, biscuits and sweets, and dried fruit and nuts. A few larger towns and resorts, like Blanes, Lloret de Mar and Palafrugell, have daily produce markets from Monday to Saturday, but these are the main weekly market days:

CENTRAL COSTA BRAVA

Banyoles – Wed
Begur – Wed
Besalú – Tue
La Bisbal – Fri
L'Estartit – Thu
Olot – Mon
Palafrugell – Sun
Ripoll – Sat
Sant Joan de les
  Abadesses – Sun
Torroella de Montgrí
  Mon

THE NORTH COAST & BEYOND

Cadaqués – Mon
Castelló d'Empúries – Tue
L'Escala – Sun
Llançà – Wed
Figueres – Thu
El Port de la Selva – Fri
Roses – Sun

THE SOUTH COAST & BEYOND

Blanes – Mon
Caldes de Malavella – Tue
Calonge – Thu
Lloret de Mar – Tue
Palamós – Tue
Platja d'Aro – Fri
Sant Feliu de Guíxols – Sun
Tossa de Mar – Thu
Vic – Tue/Sat

FISH AUCTIONS

A visit to a fish auction in one of the Costa Brava's ports can be a memorable experience – it's not all just sun and fun. Most take place at around 5pm, when the fishing fleet returns. You can see fish auctions on weekday afternoons in Blanes, L'Escala, Palamós and Roses, in the market halls adjoining each of their fishing harbours.

Food & Drink

The old towns of Girona, Figueres, Olot and Vic are full of speciality food shops – butchers, bakers, delicatessens, pâtisseries. The Catalans take great pride in their traditional foods, and even everyday items like bread and cheese are likely to have been produced by master artisans. Good buys include local sausages, Spanish hams and cheeses, olive oil, wine vinegar, Spanish wines and brandies and anchovies from L'Escala. Those with a sweet tooth should look out for *music*, a fruit and nut cake, and *torró*, a honey and nougat sweetmeat.

BESALÚ

EL REBOST DEL COMTAT
A museum of local history and crafts with a cheese and sausage shop attached, where you can taste before you buy.
✉ Plaça Llibertat 14
☎ 972 59 03 07

CASTELLFOLLIT DE LA ROCA

CAL ENRIC
This factory shop sells a tempting selection of *galetes*, delicious local biscuits made with butter and almonds. A tasty souvenir to take back home.
✉ Carretera Girona 6
☎ 972 29 40 44

MUSEU DE L'EMBOTIT
It's not everyday you visit a sausage museum (► 58), but it also sells a selection of cured meats from the Sala factory, which has been based in the village for more than 150 years.
✉ Carretera Girona 10
☎ 972 29 44 63

GIRONA

LA BODEGA
This Aladdin's cave in the old town sells wine straight from the barrel. There's also Catalan wines, spirits, olive oil and cured meats.
✉ Carrer Carreras Peralta 2
☎ 972 21 22 88

CACAO SAMPAKA
Rich chocolatey treats including truffles in a variety of unusual flavours.
✉ Carrer Santa Clara 45
☎ 972 20 23 41

J CANDELA
This shop sells *turrón* (*torró* in Catalan) produced in the family factory, as well as a range of unusual sweets.
✉ Carrer de l'Argenteria 8
☎ 972 22 09 38

GLUKI
A feast of chocolate delicacies, from chocolate teddy bears to slabs of plain, dark chocolate.
✉ Carrer Santa Clara 44
☎ 972 20 19 89

PERALADA

LA BOTIGA DEL CELLER
Wines from the castle cellars, including some fine cavas or sparkling wines.
✉ Plaça del Carme 1
☎ 972 53 80 11

OPENING HOURS

Most shops are open from around 9–1 and 5–8 Monday to Friday, and on Saturday mornings, though shops in the main tourist resorts may stay open during the afternoons and on Sundays. Markets are open in the morning, from around 8–1. The smarter clothes and craft shops are busiest in the evenings, when locals combine a spot of window-shopping with their ritual promenade.

77

Arts & Crafts

POTTERY IN LA BISBAL

The road out of La Bisbal towards Girona is lined with pottery shops selling everything from mass-produced factory pieces to innovative local designs. Among the best buys are simple earthenware cooking pots, which are both good quality and excellent value. It pays to shop around, but you are not expected to bargain. Most of these shops are open on Saturday and Sunday evenings.

LA BISBAL

AVELLÍ
Avellí is one of the biggest of La Bisbal's pottery shops. If you can't find what you are looking for here, you probably won't find it anywhere.
✉ Carrer l'Aigüeta 60–68
☎ 972 64 06 02

BAMBU BAMBU
If you can't face looking at any more pottery, this large shop on La Bisbal's 'ceramic street' has a huge collection of basketware.
✉ Carrer l'Aigüeta 61
☎ 972 64 23 33

LA BISBAL D'ART
Ceramics by local potters Pau Planes and Maria Marquès, produced at their workshop in Corça. The last pottery shop out of town on the road to Girona.
✉ Carrer l'Aigüeta 146
☎ 972 64 32 32

BOSCH
A large pottery emporium selling everyday items like earthenware plates and cooking pots at good prices.
✉ Carrer l'Aigüeta 47
☎ 972 64 39 19

LA BOTIGA
La Botiga is a pottery and gift shop with a few better pieces hidden away among the displays of tourist kitsch.
✉ Carrer l'Aigüeta 32
☎ 972 64 18 02

EL CÀNTIR
Bright, colourful, locally-made pottery sold at two shops on the main road.
✉ Carrer l'Aigüeta 45 & 126
☎ 972 64 24 72

L'ESTACIÓ
Ming-style vases, homages to the Catalan design gurus such as Miró and Picasso, and ceramic cartoon characters for children can all be found among the attractive casserole dishes and coffee pots in this eclectic pottery shop.
✉ Carrer l'Aigüeta 18
☎ 972 64 20 97

FANG
Simple but stylish hand-made pottery for the home and garden.
✉ Carrer l'Aigüeta 106
☎ 972 64 36 13

FANG I ART
All the pottery sold here is guaranteed made by hand in a local workshop. Look out for the beautiful Arab-style water-pots, which the locals fill with plants to adorn their courtyards and patios.
✉ Carrer l'Aigüeta 76
☎ 972 64 39 43

KATY
Striking and imaginative this shop sells pottery in colourful, child-like designs.
✉ Carrer l'Aigüeta 41
☎ 972 64 38 44

LLENSA
The big attraction of Llensa is the wide range of terracotta garden pots, including some antiques in a room at the back. A veritable treasure trove of pots.
✉ Carrer l'Aigüeta 91
☎ 972 64 20 71

NADAL
A retail outlet boasting a big selection of pottery for the kitchen, home and the garden.

✉ Carrer l'Aigüeta 84
☎ 972 64 03 88

D'OCC CATALONIA
Stylish, locally made ceramics and cosmetics are sold at this shop on the main street. There is another branch in Girona, at the entrance to the Jewish quarter at Carrer de la Força 1.

✉ Carrer l'Aigüeta 74
☎ 972 64 14 62

ROGENCA D'ULLASTRET
Keep walking out of town beyond the other pottery shops and you will eventually come to this one – Rogenca d'Ullastret. Everything is produced in a local workshop, and the work here is strong on individual and imaginative designs. You can also visit the workshop and exhibition room in the centre of town at Passeig Marimon Asprer 4, on the riverside promenade.

✉ Carrer l'Aigüeta 112
☎ 972 64 04 82

EL TALLERET
A range of locally produced pottery which is sold at several shops throughout this pottery town.

✉ Carrer l' Aigüeta 37, 54 & 136
☎ 972 64 27 08

VILA CLARA
This is an arty pottery workshop where everything is designed and made locally and, surprisingly, it is not as expensive as you might expect. There are two shops – one at each end of the town.

✉ Carrer l'Aigüeta 56 and Carrer Sis d'Octubre 27
☎ 972 64 25 79

PALAFRUGELL

PLATS I OLLES
An interesting shop with a good range of locally produced artefacts and gifts, mostly in ceramics and glass.

✉ Carrer Cavallers 33
☎ 972 30 01 47

PALS

PAU PLANES
As well as their pottery shop in La Bisbal, Pau Planes and Maria Marquès produce distinctive modern designs in the town of Pals, too.

✉ Plaça Major 9
☎ 972 63 64 02

PERATALLADA

LES VOLTES
Glass and pottery for sale, beneath the arches in the square.

✉ Plaça de les Voltes ☎ 972 63 41 21

TORROELLA DE MONTGRÍ

EMBOLIC
You can watch the beautiful tapestries being woven at this workshop close to the old town walls. Tapestry work makes a change from ceramics.

✉ Avinguda Lluís Companys 22
☎ 972 75 85 71

SHOPPING IN GIRONA

The streets between the Rambla and the Jewish quarter are full of small, arty boutiques, specialising in everything from ceramics to candles and religious sculpture to Carnival masks. Among the best streets for browsing are Carrer de l'Argenteria, Carrer de les Ballesteries and Carrer dels Mercaders. On the west bank, try the shops along Carrer Nou and Carrer Santa Clara for contemporary fashions and shoes. The Catalan government bookshop at Gran Via de Jaume I 38 has a wide range of books, maps and dictionaries.

Music & Festivals

THE *SARDANA*

Catalonia's national dance, in which men and women hold hands alternately around a circle, has been in existence for at least 500 years, but the modern form was invented in the 19th century. Banned during Franco's rule, it has recently been revived and the circle is seen as representing the unity of the Catalan people. *Sardana* dances, accompanied by an 11-piece orchestra called a *cobla*, are often performed in village squares on Sundays and festival days, and anyone is welcome to join in.

AUDITORI DE GIRONA

Girona's new auditorium opened in 2006 in a magnificent setting beside the River Ter. It puts on a range of classical and jazz concerts throughout the year, and is also one of the venues for the festival of world and religious music each July.
☎ 872 08 07 09,
www. auditorigirona.org

Every summer the Costa Brava plays host to a number of music festivals, with concerts of classical, jazz and pop music taking place in monasteries, churches and castles. Some of the festivals, like those at Peralada and Torroella de Montgrí, attract internationally famous artists, like the Catalan opera singers Montserrat Caballé and José Carreras; others provide a platform for local musicians. For more information on music festivals, contact the local tourist office.

CALELLA DE PALAFRUGELL

A festival of *havaneres* (► 22) is held on the beach on the first weekend in July, and the Costa Brava jazz festival takes place in the gardens of Cap Roig throughout July and August. There are also festivals of *havaneres* in the neighbouring resorts of Llafranc (► 52) and Tamariu (► 53).
☎ 972 30 02 28

CALONGE

Concerts are held in the medieval castle each July.
☎ 972 66 17 14

CASTELLÓ D'EMPÚRIES

Music festival in the cathedral in August and a festival of minstrels, with traditional Catalan songs, on 11 September.
☎ 972 15 62 33

FIGUERES

A music festival takes place each August and September in the old monastery and church of Vilabertran.
☎ 972 50 01 17

PERALADA

Top international performers appear each July and August in evening concerts in the grounds of the moated Renaissance castle.
☎ 972 53 82 92

OLOT

The biggest *sardana* festival in Catalonia (see panel) takes place in Olot on the second Sunday of July ,and features up to 5,000 dancers.
☎ 972 26 01 41

SANT FELIU DE GUÍXOLS

One of the top festivals on the Costa Brava, with international musicians appearing at concerts in the parish church in July and August.
☎ 972 82 00 51

TORROELLA DE MONTGRÍ

The international music festival which takes place between July and August in this important venue with performances ranging from chamber music to jazz. Locations for events are the town square and the Gothic church of Sant Genís.
☎ 972 76 10 98

Nightlife

BARS AND CLUBS

CADAQUÉS

L'HOSTAL

Jazz club where Salvador Dalí famously spent an evening with Mick Jagger and Gabriel García Márquez, and still the in place to meet.

✉ Passeig del Mar 8 ☎ 972 25 80 00 🕐 11am–5am daily in summer; 5pm–5am winter weekends

GIRONA

CITY ARMS

One of a chain of English-style pubs attracting a young, student crowd. There are others in the towns of Banyoles, Olot, Roses and Sant Feliu de Guíxols.

✉ Carrer Riu Güell 1
☎ 626 48 03 79

EXCALIBUR

'Celtic ale house' in the old town; locals and visitors meet to drink British beers. A taste of home shared with Spanish friends.

✉ Plaça de l'Oli 1
☎ 972 20 82 53

SALA DE BALL

Dance hall and nightclub where the locals dance the tango to live orchestras at weekends.

✉ Passeig de la Devesa
☎ 972 20 14 39

SUNSET JAZZ CLUB

Smoky jazz bar with live modern jazz on Saturday and Sunday nights.

✉ Carrer Jaume Pons i Martí 6
☎ 872 08 01 45

LLORET DE MAR

CALA BANYS

A ten-minute walk on the cliff path leads to this fashionable cocktail bar overlooking a rocky cove.

✉ Cala Banys ☎ 972 36 55 15 🕐 Daily May–Sep, 10am–3am ; Mar–Apr and Oct, Mon–Fri 10–9, Sat–Sun 10am–3am

CASINOS

Gambling was illegal in Spain during the Franco era, but the casinos are now operating again and there are two on the Costa Brava. Smart dress, including a jacket and tie for men, is obligatory; you'll also need your passport to play. A new Gran Casino de Costa Brava is scheduled to open at Lloret de Mar in 2008.

LLORET DE MAR

CASINO DE LLORET

Modern casino with gaming machines, blackjack, roulette and Spanish card games; dinner-dance and cabaret each Saturday evening.

✉ Carretera dels Esports 1
☎ 972 36 61 16 🕐 Sun–Thu 7pm–3am, Fri–Sat 7pm–4am

PERALADA

CASINO CASTELL DE PERALADA

Tapestries line the walls of this castle where you can play roulette, blackjack or *boule* in an atmosphere of elegance and fine dining.

✉ Castell de Peralada
☎ 972 53 81 25 🕐 Mon–Thu 7pm–4am, Fri–Sat 7pm–5am, Sun 5pm–5am

DISCOS

The mega-resorts of Lloret de Mar and Platja d'Aro are the nightlife hotspots of the Costa Brava. During the summer 'PR' people for the top discos tour the streets handing out free tickets to anyone deemed sufficiently young, sexy and hip. Disco fashions change with the seasons, but long-time favourites include Joy at Platja d'Aro and Tropics at Lloret de Mar. Most discos get busy around midnight and close at around 5am.

Golf

CYCLING

Bicycles can be rented in many of the coastal resorts for a gentle ride along the promenade. For something more challenging, cycle the *Vías Verdes* (greenways) on Catalonia's disused railway lines. There are three greenways in the Costa Brava region – from Olot to Girona, Girona to Sant Feliu de Guíxols, and the short 'iron route' between Ripoll and Sant Joan de les Abadesses.

The Costa Brava is emerging as a major year-round golf destination, with 10 courses open and more under construction. Clubs and trolleys are available for rent at all courses. A recent development in Catalonia is the growing popularity of pitch and putt, with shorter holes of around 100m but with the same high standards of course design and management.

GOLF COURSES

CLUB DE GOLF COSTA BRAVA
✉ Santa Cristina d'Aro, near Platja d'Aro ☎ 972 83 71 50

CLUB DE GOLF D'ARO-MASNOU
✉ Platja d'Aro ☎ 972 82 69 00

CLUB DE GOLF GIRONA
✉ Sant Julià de Ramis, near Girona ☎ 972 17 16 41

EMPORDÀ GOLF CLUB
✉ Gualta, near Torroella de Montgrí ☎ 972 76 04 50

GOLF PLATJA DE PALS
✉ Platja de Pals
☎ 972 66 77 39

GOLF SERRES DE PALS
✉ Platja de Pals
☎ 972 63 73 75

L'ANGEL DE LLORET
✉ Lloret de Mar
☎ 972 36 85 33

PERALADA GOLF CLUB
✉ Peralada ☎ 972 53 82 87

PGA GOLF DE CATALUNYA
✉ Caldes de Malavella
☎ 972 47 25 77

TORREMIRONA GOLF CLUB
✉ Navata, between Figueres and Besalú ☎ 972 55 37 37

PITCH & PUTT

GOLF CENTRE SOLIUS
✉ Santa Cristina d'Aro, near Platja d'Aro ☎ 972 83 70 59

GOLF PAPALÚS LLORET
✉ Lloret de Mar
☎ 972 36 03 14

MAS PAGÈS
✉ Sant Esteve de Guialbes, near Banyoles ☎ 972 56 10 01

PITCH & PUTT CASTELLÓ-EMPURIABRAVA
✉ Castelló d'Empúries
☎ 972 15 62 10

PITCH & PUTT ECOGOLF LLORET
✉ Lloret de Mar
☎ 972 37 10 77

PITCH & PUTT FORNELLS
✉ Fornells de la Selva, near Girona ☎ 972 47 66 72

PITCH & PUTT FRANCIAC
✉ Caldes de Malavella
☎ 972 47 10 28

PITCH & PUTT GUALTA
✉ Gualta, near Torroella de Montgrí ☎ 972 76 03 38

PITCH & PUTT GOLF PERALADA
✉ Peralada ☎ 972 53 82 87

PITCH & PUTT PLATJA D'ARO
✉ Platja d'Aro
☎ 972 81 98 20

Water Sports

The calm waters and mild climate of the Catalan coast make it ideal for water sports, the only real hazard being the *tramuntana* wind from the north. Experienced sailors can explore the Costa Brava's many sheltered coves, while beginners can develop their skills at the larger beaches on the south coast. Windsurfing, waterskiing, parascending and dinghy-sailing lessons are available at all the main resorts, as well as at Banyoles Lake, Spain's leading inland water sports location and scene of the rowing competitions during the 1992 Olympics in Barcelona. For a gentler, less energetic ride you can rent pedal boats, inflatables and canoes on all the main beaches.

MARINAS

The Costa Brava is a popular stopping-off point for yachting folk in the Mediterranean. The following marinas all have mooring and repair services available, though it is essential to book well ahead during the summer months. It is also possible to charter yachts at most of these ports.

AIGUABLAVA
62 moorings.
☎ 972 62 24 49

BLANES
320 moorings.
☎ 972 33 05 52

CALA CANYELLES (LLORET DE MAR)
130 moorings.
☎ 972 36 88 18

COLERA
150 moorings.
☎ 972 38 90 95

EMPÚRIABRAVA
5,000 moorings.
☎ 972 45 12 39

L'ESCALA
825 moorings.
☎ 972 77 00 16

L'ESTARTIT
738 moorings.
☎ 972 75 14 02

LLAFRANC
140 moorings.
☎ 972 30 07 54

LLANÇÀ
500 moorings.
☎ 972 38 07 10

PALAMÓS
867 moorings.
☎ 972 60 10 00

PLATJA D'ARO
830 moorings.
☎ 972 81 89 29

EL PORT DE LA SELVA
328 moorings.
☎ 972 38 70 00

PORTBOU
250 moorings.
☎ 972 39 07 12

ROSES
485 moorings.
☎ 972 15 44 12

SANT FELIU DE GUÍXOLS
260 moorings.
☎ 972 32 17 00

SANTA MARGARIDA (ROSES)
1,100 moorings.
☎ 972 25 77 00

SCUBA-DIVING

The clear waters of the Costa Brava make for excellent diving, especially around the Illes Medes near L'Estartit and the Illes Formigues between Palamós and Calella de Palafrugell. Diving schools in L'Estartit and Calella de Palafrugell can get you to the islands, and also offer one-day scuba-diving courses for beginners. All divers are required to take out insurance and are forbidden to fly for 24 hours after a dive.

COSTA BRAVA
practical matters

WHAT YOU NEED

	Some countries require a passport to remain valid for a minimum period (usually at least six months) beyond the date of entry – contact their consulate or embassy or your travel agent for details.	UK	Germany	USA	Netherlands	Spain
● Required ○ Suggested ▲ Not required						
Passport/National Identity Card		●	●	●	●	●
Visa (regulations can change – check before you travel)		▲	▲	▲	▲	▲
Onward or Return Ticket		▲	▲	▲	▲	▲
Health Inoculations		○	○	○	○	○
Health Documentation (reciprocal agreement: ➤ 90, Health)		●	●	▲	●	●
Travel Insurance		●	●	●	●	●
Driving Licence (non-EU nationals require an international driving licence)		●	●	●	●	●
Car Insurance Certificate (if own car)		●	●	●	●	●
Car Registration Document (if own car)		●	●	●	●	●

WHEN TO GO

Average figures for Costa Brava

High season

Low season

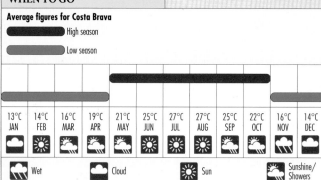

13°C JAN	14°C FEB	16°C MAR	19°C APR	21°C MAY	25°C JUN	27°C JUL	27°C AUG	25°C SEP	22°C OCT	16°C NOV	14°C DEC

🌧 Wet   ☁ Cloud   ☀ Sun   🌦 Sunshine/ Showers

TIME DIFFERENCES

GMT 12 noon	Costa Brava 1pm	Germany 1pm	USA (NY) 7am	Netherlands 1pm	Spain 1pm

TOURIST OFFICES

In the UK
Spanish Tourist Office
PO Box 4009
London, W1A 6NB
☎ (020) 7486 8077
www.tourspain.co.uk

In the USA
Tourist Office of Spain
666 Fifth Avenue
(35th Floor)
New York
NY10103
☎ (212) 265 8822
Fax: (212) 265 8864

Tourist Office of Spain
8383 Wilshire Boulevard
Suite 960
Beverley Hills
CA 90211
☎ (323) 658 7192
Fax: (323) 658 1061
www.spain.info

ARRIVING

Girona-Costa Brava airport is served by regular flights from London and other European cities. There are several flights a day from the UK operated by Ryanair (www.ryanair.com). Shuttle buses connect the airport with the city centre and main tourist resorts. A wider range of airlines serves Barcelona airport, 100km south.

Barcelona (El Prat) Airport
Kilometres to Girona

100 kilometres

Journey times
🚌 2 hours
🚆 N/A
🚗 90 minutes

Girona-Costa Brava Airport
Kilometres to Girona

11 kilometres

Journey times
🚌 N/A
🚆 30 minutes 20 minutes
🚗

MONEY

Spain's currency is the euro (€) which is divided into 100 cents. Coins come in denominations of 1, 2, 5, 10, 20 and 50 cents, and notes come in 5, 10, 20, 50, 100, 200 and 500 euro denominations (the last two are rarely seen). The notes and one side of the coins are the same throughout the European single currency zone. Notes and coins from any of the other countries can be used in Spain.
Major credit cards are widely accepted. Certain credit and debit cards can be also be used to withdraw euro notes from ATMs, which are widely distributed in major towns and resorts.

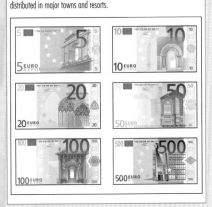

TIME

 Like the rest of Spain, Catalonia is one hour ahead of Greenwich Mean Time (GMT+1), except from late March to late October, when summer time (GMT+2) operates.

CUSTOMS

 YES

From another EU country for personal use (guidelines)
800 cigarettes, 200 cigars,
1 kilogram of tobacco
10 litres of spirits (over 22%)
20 litres of aperitifs
90 litres of wine, of which 60 litres can be sparkling wine
110 litres of beer

From a non-EU country for your personal use, the allowances are:
200 cigarettes OR
50 cigars OR
250 grams of tobacco
1 litre of spirits (over 22%)
2 litres of intermediary products (eg sherry) and sparkling wine
2 litres of still wine
50 grams of perfume
0.25 litres of eau de toilette

Travellers under 17 years of age are not entitled to the tobacco and alcohol allowances.

 NO

Drugs, firearms, ammunition, offensive weapons, obscene material, unlicensed animals.

CONSULATES

UK
☎ 933 66 62 00

Germany
☎ 932 92 10 00

USA
☎ 932 80 22 27

Netherlands
☎ 934 10 62 10

TOURIST OFFICES

- **Blanes**
  Passeig de Catalunya 2
  ☎ 972 33 03 48

- **Figueres**
  Placa del Sol
  ☎ 972 50 31 55

- **Girona**
  Rambla de la Llibertat 1
  ☎ 972 22 65 75

- **Lloret de Mar**
  Passeig Camprodón i Arrieta 1
  ☎ 972 36 47 35

- **Olot**
  Carrer del'Hospici 8
  ☎ 972 26 01 41

- **Palafrugell**
  Placa del'Església
  ☎ 972 30 02 28

- **Tossa de Mar**
  Avinguda del Pelegrí 25
  ☎ 972 34 01 08

- **Vic**
  Carrer Ciutat 4
  ☎ 938 86 20 91

The above offices are open throughout the year. Most towns and villages have offices open in summer; look out for the international 🛈 sign.

The staff are usually multilingual and helpful and can supply you with local maps and guides.

Information about the Costa Brava can also be found at www.costabrava.org

NATIONAL HOLIDAYS

J	F	M	A	M	J	J	A	S	O	N	D
2		2	(2)	1	1		1	1	1	1	4

1 Jan	New Year's Day
6 Jan	Epiphany
Mar/Apr	Good Friday, Easter Monday
1 May	Labour Day
24 Jun	St John's Day
15 Aug	Assumption of the Virgin
11 Sep	Catalan National Day
12 Oct	Spanish National Day
1 Nov	All Saints' Day
6 Dec	Constitution Day
8 Dec	Feast of the Immaculate Conception
25 Dec	Christmas Day
26 Dec	St Stephen's Day

OPENING HOURS

○ Shops	● Post Offices
● Offices	◐ Museums
● Banks	◐ Pharmacies

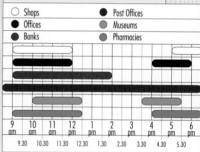

9 am	10 am	11 am	12 pm	1 pm	2 pm	3 pm	4 pm	5 pm	6 pm
9.30	10.30	11.30	12.30	1.30	2.30	3.30	4.30	5.30	

Most shops close on Saturday evening and all day on Sunday, though supermarkets and shops in the larger resorts may be open throughout the day seven days a week. Banks open Saturday mornings in the winter only. There will always be one pharmacist on duty in the main towns and the details will be published in local papers and shop windows.
Individual museum opening hours are listed throughout the guide. Many museums close on Mondays, except on national holidays when they follow Sunday hours.

ELECTRICITY

The power supply in Spain is 220–225 volts. Sockets accept two-round-pin style plugs.

Visitors from the UK require an adaptor.

Vistors from the US require a transformer for appliances operating on 100–120 volts.

TIPS/GRATUITIES

Yes ✓   No ✗

Restaurants	✓	10%
Cafés/bars	✓	change
Taxis	✓	10%
Tour guides	✓	€1–2
Porters	✓	€1–2
Chambermaids	✓	€1–2
Hairdressers	✓	€1–2
Restroom attendants	✓	change
Toilets	✗	

PUBLIC TRANSPORT

Trains

The main line from Barcelona to France passes through the Costa Brava region, with regular stops at Girona, Figueres and Portbou. There is also a branch line linking Barcelona and Girona with Blanes. For information on train services, call RENFE on ☎ 902 24 02 02; www.renfe.es

Buses

A wide network of local bus routes, operated by a number of private companies, the largest being Sarfa, connects Girona and Figueres with the main towns and villages of the Costa Brava. Extra routes connect the coastal resorts in summer. Timetables change, so check with your local tourist office or at the nearest bus station.

Boats

A regular boat service connects the resorts of Blanes, Lloret de Mar and Tossa de Mar between April and October, with some boats continuing north as far as Palamós. There are departures at least hourly, calling at various beaches along the way, so you can use this service for day-trips to nearby beaches and coves. There are also a number of cruises in summer from all the major resorts, including Cadaqués, Roses, Empúriabrava, L'Estartit and Sant Feliu de Guíxols – details can be found on the quayside at noticeboards and ticket kiosks. One popular trip is the cruise to the Medes islands on a glass-hulled boat from L'Estartit (► D3).

Internal Flights

You can fly to Madrid and the Balearic Islands direct from Girona-Costa Brava airport. To fly to other major cities within Spain you will find Barcelona airport provides a more comprehensive service.

CAR RENTAL

The leading inter-national car rental companies have offices at Barcelona and Girona airports.
There are local car rental companies in the resorts. Keep the rental documents, your driving licence and your passport with you at all times.

TAXIS

Taxis can be rented at ranks or by flagging down a taxi with a green light on the roof. Prices are good, but there are supplements for late night, weekend and public holiday travel, as well as for luggage and long-distance journeys, so check in advance.

CONCESSIONS

Students/Youths Holders of an International Student Identity Card (ISIC) may be able to obtain some concessions on travel and entrance fees. Anyone under 26 or belonging to a national youth hostel organi-sation can stay cheaply at the hostels (*albergues de joventut*) in Girona, Banyoles, Olot and Empúries.

Senior Citizens There are few specific discounts available for senior citizens, though it is always worth checking at museums and tourist attrac-tions. A number of hotels and tour operators offer economical deals on long-stay winter holidays, when the savings in the cost of fuel bills can almost wipe out the cost of the trip.

DRIVING

Speed limit on motorways (*autopistas* – toll payable) 120kph

Speed limit on main roads: 100kph (on minor roads 90kph)

Speed limit on urban roads: 50kph

Seat belts must be worn at all times. Children under 12 must use an approved child seat/harness.

Random breath-testing. Never drive under the influence of alcohol.

Fuel (*gasolina*) is sold in various grades, including unleaded (*sense plomb*) and super-unleaded and diesel (*gasoil*). A few petrol stations are self-service but most have an attendant. Credit cards are widely accepted and at some you can pay at the pump using your card.

If you are driving your own car in Spain it is a good idea to take out European breakdown cover before you leave. Members of AIT-affiliated motoring clubs, including the AA, can use the services of the Real Automóvil Club de España (RACE ☎ 902 40 45 45). Car-retnal firms provide their own rescue service.

PHOTOGRAPHY

What to photograph: rocky coastline, wild flowers, Romanesque churches, the old towns of Girona and Tossa de Mar.
Best time to photograph: early morning and evening, when the sunlight is subtle rather than overpowering.
Where to buy film: film and camera batteries are widely available in pharmacies (*farmàcias*) and also in many tourist shops.

PERSONAL SAFETY

In an emergency, ask for the nearest police station (*comissaria*) and speak to the Policía Nacional, known in Catalonia as the Mossos d'Esquadra. Take sensible precautions to avoid crime.

- Don't carry more cash than you need.
- Never leave valuables on the beach or by the pool.
- Always lock your car with any valuables out of sight in the boot.
- Beware of pickpockets in crowded markets or tourist sights.

Tourist Police assistance:
☎ **112**
from any call box

TELEPHONES

Public telephones take euro coins as well as phonecards (*teletarjetas*) which can be bought at post offices or tobacconists. Most also accept credit cards. The cheap rate for international calls is weekdays 10pm–8am, after 2pm Sat and all day Sun.

International Dialling Codes	
From Spain to:	
UK:	00 44
Germany:	00 49
USA:	00 1
Netherlands:	00 31

POST

Post Offices

Post offices (*Correus*) are generally open Monday to Saturday 9am–1pm. Stamps (*segells*) can also be bought at kiosks and at *estancs* (tobacconists' shops). The main post office is in Girona, on Avinguda Roman Folch; it is open Monday to Saturday 8am–9pm.

HEALTH

Medical Treatment
Citizens of European Union (EU) countries are entitled to receive free health care in Spain on production of their European Health Insurance Card (EHIC). However, this only covers essential treatment and private medical insurance is still advisable.

Dental Services
Dental treatment is rarely covered by reciprocal health care agreements as most dentists only practise privately. Emergency dental treatment should be covered by private medical insurance.

Sun Advice
Visitors from non-Mediterranean climates can burn quickly in the summer sun. It is best to avoid the midday sun altogether and to use a high-factor sun block, especially at first. Children are particularly vulnerable to the sun and should always wear a hat.

Drugs
Prescription and non-prescription drugs are available from pharmacies (*farmàcies*), distinguished by a large green cross. Recreational drugs, which you may be offered at nightclubs in the larger resorts, are illegal and should be avoided.

Safe Water
Tap water is generally safe to drink, but mineral water is cheap and easy to buy, either sparkling (*amb gas*) or still (*sense gas*). Remember, drink plenty of water to avoid dehydration.

LANGUAGE

Since 1979 Catalan (Català) has returned to being the official language of Catalonia, and although Spanish is still universally understood, it is Catalan that you are most likely to see and hear on the streets. A Romance language, with its roots in ancient Latin, it is spoken in Valencia, Andorra, the Balearic islands and parts of the French Pyrenees, as well as in Catalonia. Many Catalan words look like their equivalents in French or Spanish – but the sound of the language (definitely not a dialect of Spanish) is utterly distinct.

hotel	hotel	toilet	vàter
campsite	càmping	balcony	balcó
apartment	apartament	sea view	vista al mar
single room	habitació senzilla	one night	una nit
double room	habitació doble	breakfast	esmorzar
bath	bany	key	clau
shower	dutxa	lift	ascensor
washbasin	lavabo	stairs	escala

bank	banc	credit card	carta de crèdit
exchange bureau	oficina de canvi	change	canvi
cashier	caixer	how much?	quant és?
travellers' cheque	xec de viatge	expensive	car
foreign currency	moneda estrangera	cheap	bon preu
banknote	bitllet de banc	post office	correus

lunch	dinar	water	aigua
dinner	sopar	...sparkling	...amb gas
menu	carta	...still	...sense gas
set menu	menú	beer	cervesa
waiter	cambrer	draught beer	una canya
waitress	cambrera	dessert	postre
white wine	vi blanc	coffee	café
red wine	vi negre	the bill	el compte

airport	aeroport	taxi	taxi
aeroplane	avió	car	cotxe
station	estació	garage	garatge
train	tren	petrol station	gasolinera
bus	autobús	petrol	gasolina
boat	vaixell	...unleaded	...sense plomb
ticket	bitllet	motorway	autopista
return	anar i tornar	bicycle	bicicleta

yes	sí	excuse me	perdoni
no	no	sorry	ho sento
please	sisplau	welcome	benvinguts
thank you	gràcies	open	obert
hello	hola	closed	tancat
good morning	bon dia	do you speak English?	parla anglès?
good afternoon	bona tarda	I don't speak Catalan	no parlo català
goodnight	bona nit	I don't understand	no ho entenc
goodbye	adéu		

REMEMBER

- To contact your airline or your tour operator on the day before leaving to confrm flight details.
- To arrive at the airport at least two hours before your flight, leaving time to return your rental car if necessary.
- The shops at Barcelona airport sell a wide range of alcohol, tobacco, gifts, perfumes, fashions, jewellery, music and toys.

Index

TwinPack
Costa Brava

Written and updated by Tony Kelly
Produced by AA Publishing
Editorial management Apostrophe S Limited
Designer Jacqueline Bailey
Series editor Cathy Hatley

A CIP catalogue record for this book is available from the British Library.

ISBN 978-0-7495-5540-5

Material in this book may have appeared in other AA publications.

Published by AA Publishing, a trading name of Automobile Association Developments Limited, whose registered address is Fanum House, Basing View, Basingstoke, Hampshire, RG21 4EA. Registered number 1878835.

Colour separation by Keenes, Andover
Printed and bound by Everbest Printing Co. Ltd, China

ACKNOWLEDGEMENTS
The Automobile Association would like to thank the following photographers, companies and picture libraries for their assistance in the preparation of this book. Abbreviations for the picture credits are as follows: (t) top; (b) bottom; (l) left; (r) right; (AA) AA World Travel Library.

1 AA/M Chaplow; 5t AA/M Chaplow; 5b AA/P Enticknap; 6 AA/M Chaplow; 7t, 7b AA/M Chaplow; 9 Illustrated London News; 12t, 12b AA/M Chaplow; 13t, 13b AA/M Chaplow; 14 AA/M Chaplow; 15 AA/M Chaplow; 16 AA/M Chaplow; 17 AA/M Chaplow; 18 AA/M Chaplow; 19 AA/M Chaplow; 20 AA/M Chaplow; 21t, 21b AA/M Chaplow; 23t AA/P Enticknap; 23b AA/M Chaplow; 24t AA/P Enticknap; 24b AA/M Chaplow; 25t AA/P Enticknap; 25b AA/M Chaplow; 26t, 26b AA/M Chaplow; 27t, 27b AA/M Chaplow; 28t AA/M Chaplow; 28b AA/P Enticknap; 29t Arco Images/Alamy; 29b T Vilches/Alamy; 30t, 30b AA/M Chaplow; 31t, 31b AA/M Chaplow; 32t, 32b AA/M Chaplow; 33t AA/M Chaplow; 33b AA/P Enticknap; 34t, 34b AA/M Chaplow; 35t AA/M Chaplow; 35b I Dagnall/Alamy; 36t, 36b AA/M Chaplow; 37t, 37b AA/M Chaplow; 38t, 38b C Pillitz/Alamy; 39t, 39b AA/M Chaplow; 40t AA/P Enticknap; 40b AA/P Enticknap; 41t, 41b AA/M Chaplow; 42t, 42l AA/M Chaplow; 43t, 43b AA/M Chaplow; 44t AA/P Enticknap; 44b AA/M Chaplow; 45t AA/S Watkins; 45b AA/M Chaplow; 46t, 46b AA/M Chaplow; 47t AA/S Watkins; 47b AA/M Chaplow; 48t, 48b AA/M Chaplow; 49t, 49b AA/M Chaplow; 50 AA/M Chaplow; 51 AA/M Chaplow; 52 AA/M Chaplow; 53 AA/M Chaplow; 54 AA/M Chaplow; 56 AA/M Chaplow; 57 Water World; 58 AA/ Chaplow; 59 AA/M Chaplow; 60 AA/M Chaplow; 61t, 61b AA/M Chaplow; 84 AA/M Chaplow; 85t, 85b AA/M Chaplow; 90t, 90c AA/M Chaplow; 90cl AA/M Jourdan.

Front cover, left to right: AA/M Chaplow (a) Dalí statue; (b) yacht; (c) wine; (d) church, Lloret de Mar; (f) market stall holder; (g) Catalan salad; AA/P Enticknap (e) flower. Back cover, top to bottom: AA/M Chaplow (a) Monestir de Santa Maria, Ripoll; (b) pots; (c) café; Brand X Pictures (d) dancers.

Every effort has been made to trace the copyright holders, and we apologise in advance for any accidental errors. We would be happy to apply the corrections in the following edition of this publication.

A03195
Maps in this title produced from map data supplied by Global Mapping, Brackley, UK.
Licence No – 07/021. Copyright © Global Mapping/Cartografia 2007

TITLES IN THE TWINPACK SERIES
• Algarve • Andalucía • Corfu • Costa Blanca • Costa Brava • Costa del Sol • Crete •
• Croatia • Cyprus • Dubai • Gran Canaria • Lanzarote & Fuerteventura • Madeira •
• Mallorca • Malta & Gozo • Menorca • Provence & the Côte d'Azur • Tenerife •

Dear **TwinPack** Traveller

Your comments, opinions and recommendations are very important to us. So please help us to improve our travel guides by taking a few minutes to complete this simple questionnaire.

You do not need a stamp (unless posted outside the UK). If you do not want to cut this page from your guide, then photocopy it or write your answers on a plain sheet of paper.

Send to: **The Editor, AA TwinPack Travel Guides, FREEPOST SCE 4598, Basingstoke RG21 4GY.**

Your recommendations…

We always encourage readers' recommendations for restaurants, nightlife or shopping – if your recommendation is used in the next edition of the guide, we will send you a **FREE AA TwinPack Guide** of your choice. Please state below the establishment name, location and your reasons for recommending it.

_____
_____
_____
_____

Please send me **AA TwinPack**

Algarve ❏ Andalucía ❏ Corfu ❏ Costa Blanca ❏
Costa Brava ❏ Costa del Sol ❏ Crete ❏ Croatia ❏
Cyprus ❏ Dubai ❏ Gran Canaria ❏ Lanzarote & Fuerteventura ❏
Madeira ❏ Mallorca ❏ Malta & Gozo ❏ Menorca ❏
Provence & the Côte d'Azur ❏ Tenerife ❏
(please tick as appropriate)

About this guide…

Which title did you buy?
AA *TwinPack* _____
Where did you buy it? _____
When? m m / y y

Why did you choose an AA *TwinPack* Guide? _____
_____
_____
_____

Did this guide meet your expectations?
Exceeded ❏   Met all ❏   Met most ❏   Fell below ❏
Please give your reasons _____
_____
_____

continued on next page…

Were there any aspects of this guide that you particularly liked? _____

_____

_____

Is there anything we could have done better? _____

_____

_____

About you…

Name *(Mr/Mrs/Ms)* _____

Address _____

_____

_____ Postcode _____

Daytime tel no _____

Please only give us your mobile phone number if you wish to hear from us about other products and services from the AA and partners by text or mms.

Which age group are you in?

Under 25 ☐   25–34 ☐   35–44 ☐   45–54 ☐   55–64 ☐   65+ ☐

How many trips do you make a year?

None ☐   One ☐   Two ☐   Three or more ☐

Are you an AA member? Yes ☐   No ☐

About your trip…

When did you book? m m / y y   When did you travel? m m / y y

How long did you stay? _____

Was it for business or leisure? _____

Did you buy any other travel guides for your trip?

If yes, which ones? _____

Thank you for taking the time to complete this questionnaire. Please send it to us as soon as possible, and remember, you do not need a stamp *(unless posted outside the UK)*.

Happy Holidays!

The information we hold about you will be used to provide the products and services requested and for identification, account administration, analysis, and fraud/loss prevention purposes. More details about how that information is used is in our privacy statement, which you'll find under the heading "Personal Information" in our terms and conditions and on our website: www.theAA.com. Copies are also available from us by post, by contacting the Data Protection Manager at AA, Fanum House, Basing View, Basingstoke, Hampshire RG21 4EA.

We may want to contact you about other products and services provided by us, or our partners (by mail, telephone) but please tick the box if you DO NOT wish to hear about such products and services from us by mail or telephone. ☐